ON THEIR OWN

ON THEIR OWN

Shipwrecks & Survivals

MERVYN HORDER

Duckworth

First published in 1988 by
Gerald Duckworth & Co. Ltd.
The Old Piano Factory
43 Gloucester Crescent, London NW1

ISBN 0 7156 1016 3

British Library Cataloguing in Publication Data

Horder, Mervyn
    On their own : shipwrecks and survivals.
    1. Shipwrecks   2. Yachts and yachting
    3. Survival (after airplane accidents,
    shipwrecks, etc.)
    I. Title
    910.4'53   G525

    ISBN 0-7156-1016-3

Photoset in North Wales by
Derek Doyle & Associates, Mold, Clwyd
and printed in Great Britain by
Biddles Ltd, Guildford and King's Lynn

Contents

Preface

A shipwreck book published in Edinburgh in 1812 carries on its title-page, in the manner of the age, a flowery subtitle: *Historical Narratives of the Most Noted Calamities and Providential Deliveries which have resulted from Maritime Enterprise, with a sketch of Various Expedients for Preserving the Life of the Mariners*. This, broadly speaking, is the brief of the present volume. Its intention is to salute not merely the acts of fortitude and endurance in which the stories abound, but the spirit of ingenuity and improvisation which the various wrenches of adversity, in particular the torments of hunger and thirst, have called forth – to honour, in fact, the wits as well as the guts of those caught up without warning and against their will in such great adventures.

Printed in chronological order, the stories are chosen on purpose from different parts of the world to be as varied as possible. They toe no particular line, preach no particular lesson, except the fatal consequences *always* of drinking sea water, and occasionally the regenerative effect of strongly held religious beliefs. Some of the victims have been returned to their loved ones after a few days, others have had to adapt themselves to eating the bread of exile for up to twenty years. I have omitted the *Titanic* disaster of 1912, also the whole of the Bligh of the *Bounty* story, about both of which so large and contentious a literature has already appeared. I am aware that the book is short on incidents of the First World War, perhaps too long on the seventeenth and eighteenth centuries; but this latter was the age *par excellence* of nautical expansion in not too well found, often overcrowded, sailing vessels in remote parts of the world, and it was therefore *par excellence* the age of the shipwreck.

I have extended my programme to include two stories (nos. 6 and 11) in which the irrevocable depositing of the protagonists on land was due not strictly to shipwreck but to some other kind of nautical accident; and one (no. 3) in which the principal was lured on shore from his ship by treachery. I should be sorry to omit either 3 or 11, since in both the documentation makes it possible to get closer to the characters of those taking part than in most of the other stories.

A book entirely composed of sea journeys in open boats, however heroic, might prove monotonous in the end. No less absorbing are the shifts and immediate contrivances necessary to keep going at all, the variety of answers to the question what happens next, when shipwreck victims first find themselves on land in a completely strange place, and their subsequent adventures getting home, which often call for pure patience above all other qualities. Of all the stories in the book I consider no. 12 the most astonishing for its triumph of unobtrusive leadership, no. 6 for the ingenuity of its improvisations, and no. 16 for the incredible physical endurance shown.

The more substantial pieces in this book – 2, 3, 4, 5, 10, 11, and 12 – have been written by me; the shorter ones – 1, 6, 7, 8, 9, 13, 14, 15, 16 – are reproduced verbatim from other printed sources, as acknowledged in the Bibliography and Notes. The last four – 13 to 16 – are taken from Royal Naval Intelligence summaries of the last War, and have not, so far as I know, appeared previously in any other book available to the public.

Apart from a minor incident with a crowded but leaky rowboat somewhere up in the Stockholm Archipelago one afternoon in 1937, I have never myself been within miles of being shipwrecked. My only direct link with the stories is the circumstance that Aubyn Trevor-Battye, hero of no. 11, when he retired to England at the end of his adventurous life, built in 1912, near Petersfield, Hants, the Edwardian country house Ashford Chace, which my father bought from his widow and lived in happily for the last thirty years of his life; there is more about this curious house in my memoir of my father, *The Little Genius* (Duckworth, 1966).

I cherish the hope that the reading of something somewhere

in these very varied adventures may some day help to save the life, or improve the condition, of a future shipwreck victim. Good luck to us all.

London, 1987   M.H.

1

St Paul on Melita

And when it was determined that we should sail for Italy, they delivered Paul and certain other prisoners to a centurion named Julius, of the Augustan band. And embarking in a ship of Adramyttium, which was about to sail unto the places on the coast of Asia, we put to sea, Aristarchus, a Macedonian of Thessalonica, being with us. And the next day we touched at Sidon: and Julius treated Paul kindly, and gave him leave to go unto his friends and refresh himself. And putting to sea from thence, we sailed under the lee of Cyprus, because the winds were contrary. And when we had sailed across the sea which is off Cilicia and Pamphylia, we came to Myra, *a city* of Lycia. And there the centurion found a ship of Alexandria sailing for Italy; and he put us therein. And when we had sailed slowly many days, and were come with difficulty over against Cnidus, the wind not further suffering us, we sailed under the lee of Crete, over against Salmone; and with difficulty coasting along it we came unto a certain place called Fair Havens; nigh whereunto was the city of Lasea.

And when much time was spent, and the voyage was now dangerous, because the Fast was now already gone by, Paul admonished them, and said unto them, Sirs, I perceive that the voyage will be with injury and much loss, not only of the lading and the ship, but also of our lives. But the centurion gave more heed to the master and to the owner of the ship, than to those things which were spoken by Paul. And because the haven was not commodious to winter in, the more part advised to put to sea from thence, if by any means they could reach Phoenix, and winter *there*; *which is* a haven of Crete, looking north-east and south-east. And when the south wind blew softly, supposing that they had obtained their purpose, they weighed anchor and sailed along Crete, close in shore. But after no long time there beat down from it a tempestuous wind, which is called Euraquilo; and when the ship was caught, and could not face the wind, we gave way *to it*, and were driven. And running under the lee of a small island called Cauda, we were able, with difficulty, to secure the boat; and when they had hoisted it up, they used helps, under-girding the ship; and, fearing lest they should be cast upon the Syrtis, they lowered the gear, and so were driven. And as we laboured exceedingly with the storm, the next day they began to throw *the freight* overboard; and the third day they cast out with their own hands the tackling of the ship. And when neither sun nor stars shone upon *us* for many days, and no small tempest lay on *us*, all hope that we should be saved was now taken away. And when they had been long without food, then Paul stood forth in the midst of them, and said, Sirs, ye should have hearkened unto me, and not have set sail from Crete, and have gotten this injury and loss. And now I exhort you to be of good cheer: for there shall be no loss of life among you, but *only* of the ship. For there stood by me this night an angel of the God whose I am, whom also I serve, saying, Fear not, Paul; thou must stand before Caesar: and lo, God hath granted thee all them that sail with thee. Wherefore, sirs, be of good cheer: for I believe God, that it shall be even so as it hath been spoken unto me. Howbeit we must be cast upon a certain island.

But when the fourteenth night was come, as we were driven to and fro in the *sea of* Adria, about midnight the sailors surmised that they were drawing near to some country; and they sounded, and found twenty fathoms: and after a little space, they sounded again, and found fifteen fathoms. And fearing lest haply we should be cast ashore on rocky ground they let go four anchors from the stern, and wished for the day. And as the sailors were seeking to flee out of the ship, and had lowered the boat into the sea, under colour as though they would lay out anchors from the foreship, Paul said to the centurion and to the soldiers, Except these abide in the ship, ye cannot be saved. Then the soldiers cut away the ropes of the boat, and let her fall off. And while the day was coming on, Paul besought them all to take some food, saying, This day is the fourteenth day that ye wait and continue fasting, having taken nothing. Wherefore I beseech you to take some food: for this is for your safety: for there shall not a hair perish from the head of any of you. And when he had said this, and had taken bread, he gave thanks to God in the presence of all: and he brake it, and began to eat. Then were they all of good cheer, and themselves also took food. And we were in all in the ship two hundred threescore and sixteen souls. And when they had eaten enough, they lightened the ship, throwing out the wheat into the sea. And when it was day, they knew not the land: but they perceived a certain bay with a beach, and they took counsel whether they could drive the ship upon it. And casting off the anchors, they left them in the sea, at the same time loosing the bands of the rudders; and hoisting up the foresail to the wind, they made for the beach. But lighting upon a place where two seas met, they ran the vessel aground; and the foreship struck and remained unmoveable, but the stern began to break up by the violence *of the waves*. And the soldiers' counsel was to kill the prisoners, lest any *of them* should swim out, and escape. But the centurion, desiring to save Paul, stayed them from their purpose; and commanded that they which could swim should cast themselves overboard, and get first to the land: and the rest, some on planks, and some on *other* things from the ship. And so it came to pass, that they all escaped safe to the land.

And when we were escaped, then we knew that the island was called Melita. And the barbarians shewed us no common kindness: for they kindled a fire, and received us all, because of the present rain, and because of the cold. But when Paul had gathered a bundle of sticks, and laid them on the fire, a viper came out by reason of the heat, and fastened on his hand. And when the barbarians saw the beast hanging from his hand, they said one to another, No doubt this man is a murderer, whom, though he hath escaped from the sea, yet Justice hath not suffered to live. Howbeit he shook off the beast into the fire, and took no harm. But they expected that he would have swollen, or fallen down dead suddenly: but when they were long in expectation, and beheld nothing amiss come to him, they changed their minds, and said that he was a god.

Now in the neighbourhood of that place were lands belonging to the chief man of the island, named Publius; who received us, and entertained us three days courteously. And it was so, that the father of Publius lay sick of fever and dysentery: unto whom Paul entered in, and prayed, and laying his hands on him healed him. And when this was done, the rest also which had diseases in the island came, and were cured: who also honoured us with many honours; and when we sailed, they put on board such things as we needed.

2

An Elizabethan Sailor

The papal commissions inaugurating the Spanish Inquisition were issued in September 1480, and the first two commissioners arrived in Seville on Christmas Day to begin their work. It was an institution which both answered to, and was shaped by, the deep underlying elements of cruelty in the Spanish character, and the Spanish love of display and an unexpected talent for clandestine bureaucracy; for these reasons the Inquisition in Spain was more highly organised and autonomous than the Papal Inquisition which preceded it, or than the Inquisition in any other country. Though the organisation acquired more and more civil authority as time went on, its object was primarily to ensure the purity of the Roman faith, and its principal quarries were Jews, Moslems and Protestants – among the first two, mainly those who had for various self-seeking reasons nominally embraced the Roman faith but secretly carried on their old observances. Of Protestants there were few in Spain itself, but large numbers in Holland, then a Spanish dominion; and in the 1560s a blanket Inquisition decree was actually passed, and signed by Philip II of Spain, condemning the whole population of the Netherlands, all three million of them, to death for heresy.

By 1490 there were fifteen Inquisition headquarters in Spain, ranging from the busiest ones at Seville, Toledo and Madrid down to minor branches in Catalonia and Majorca. The last-named began operations in 1488 by zealously persecuting those of Jewish origin in the islands, but – the population of the Balearics being small – probably it had not much to do after its initial burst of activity.

A hundred years later, it was into the clutches of this peripheral Inquisition outstation that, in April 1587, fell Robert Hasleton, a young British sailor from Braintree in Essex who had left England in 1582 on a ship trading to Asia Minor, and who had already endured, as a result of shipwrecks, piracy and some overt warlike acts, an amazing sequence of adventures in a Mediterranean largely under Turkish domination. Four of these years, weak, sick and miserable, he had spent chained to his oar as a galley-slave after being sold to an Algerian slave-master for sixty-six doubloons.

Not the least astonishing of his achievements, at the last of his three shipwrecks, when he was cast up on the island of Formentera, off Ibiza, one of only fifteen survivors from a ship's company of two hundred and fifty, was to manage to break his chain during the wreck and float himself ashore on an oar. Here, after knocking off the rest of his fetters against a sharp rock, and with every hope of favourable treatment at last after his years as a Moslem slave, he gave himself up to the Christian authorities, together with one of his fellow slaves who, either to curry favour or out of sheer spite, revealed to them that Hasleton was an English Lutheran. This news caused a sensation comparable to the discovery of a Hindu at the gates of Mecca; and Hasleton found himself once more in chains, shipped over to Majorca, where the captain of his ship came upon the Chief Inquisitor walking in the Palma market-place, and handed over his captive personally.

Hasleton's first interrogation lasted about a month, three or four sessions each week, in a church. At the end of the first session the Inquisitor blessed him, but never again. Hasleton returned with sustained vehemence the standard Protestant answers to the standard Roman questions. That he had not been brought up in the Roman faith, neither would he submit himself to it. That in England the Gospel was truly preached and maintained by a most gracious princess; and that he would not commit idolatry, which is condemned by the Word of God. That he had received the sacraments, but denied the process of transubstantiation. That he had confessed his sins

Richard Hasleton

to God but would never do so to any friar, since a man who is himself a sinner cannot forgive sins. That he would kneel at the altar but not pray to any images thereon, since he recognised no mediator but Jesus Christ. And when at one point the Inquisitor pressed him to lay his hands on a crucifix, Hasleton replied as directly as he could by spitting in the Inquisitor's face.

Nor, being cussed and an Englishman, was he backward in plying the Inquisitor with his own questions. Did they think him to be a true Christian? – to which the answer was 'Yes, in some respects; but you are out of the faith of the true Church'. Why, when God through His mercy had freed him from the Turks, did he now find Christians even more cruel to him? It was in answer to this last that Hasleton learned for the first time that the matters in dispute were not merely theological, but political as well: that the King of Spain was at war with Queen Elizabeth, that the Armada was even then being brought to readiness, and that, as they boastfully assured him, 'it would not be long now'. To his last question – why they thought the Roman Church should have the supremacy – the Inquisitor returned no answer at all.

At the end of the month, with the prisoner deaf to lures and threats alike, the Inquisitor's patience was exhausted and he resorted to a standard Inquisition technique – prolonged imprisonment. Hasleton was thrown into a dungeon thirty feet under the castle of Palma on a diet of a little bread and water once a day. Here he remained in solitary confinement, in the dark, for a whole year.

One day, while the jailer was out at Mass, it fell to his small son to let down to Hasleton his daily ration of bread and water, and the boy by mistake left the rope hanging in position. Hasleton saw this at once as a sign from heaven and forthwith made his escape, in a manner well-nigh incredible to us when we remember that he was weakened by a whole year's solitary confinement, but by no means the only occasion on which he showed his physical toughness. He swarmed up the rope, heaved the trapdoor open with his shoulders, hid till dark under a heap of lime stored in one of the castle rooms, then used the harness of three horses he found standing in a courtyard to fashion himself a rope which enabled him to get over the castle wall. For two hours he was at large in the streets of Palma, still deserted because of religious ceremonies – it was 1st May 1588, the feast of SS. Philip and James – then finally he got out of the city by the only means he could think of which would not bring him face to face with the guards, by diving into the main drain and being swept out through a watergate under the city's walls. He was six miles away from the city by daybreak.

In spite of the general hue and cry after him he remained at liberty for twelve days, eating berries and roots and supplementing his few rags of clothing with some pieces of stolen horse-cloth tied together with palm fibre; but he was then challenged by a passing peasant who, when Hasleton showed fight, called up some of his friends and overpowered him. Bound hand and foot to a mule Hasleton was brought back to Palma, and the Inquisitor this time ordered an iron clasp with a thirty-foot chain hanging from it to be put round his neck.

The next day they proceeded to torture him, in an underground vault with four people present, the Inquisitor, a legal officer, the torturer and a Dutchwoman to act as interpreter. He might be accounted lucky in that out of the three standard Inquisition tortures – the rack, the water torture and the *strappado*, in which the victim's limbs were dislocated by jerks with a pulley – only the first two were used against him.

After he had knelt and prayed the Lord to strengthen his faith, they tied him to the rack with ropes round his arm and thigh muscles, and put a hollow cane-funnel in his mouth. Simultaneously with the slow tightening of the ropes, by twisting them with sticks like four tourniquets, they poured water through the cane till his stomach and lungs could hold no more; and the whole time the Dutchwoman continued to exhort him to yield and confess the faith of Rome. He was so strong that at one point the rope on his left arm burst, but he continued all the time alternately to pray and to answer the Dutchwoman; until, with a new rope twisted even tighter, the pain was so great that he could no longer speak, and after one last agonised outburst he lay still as if unconscious. At this point the Dutchwoman put her hand on his head and reported that he was dead; so they untied him and left him in another room, to recover or not as the case might be.

Here he lay for five days, vomiting blood and water and incapable of taking food, but very slowly recovering, so that on the sixth day he could manage the little dole of bread soaked in wine they gave him. This saving diet was not provided through any feelings of mercy or change of heart; the very same day they propped him on a donkey and whipped him publicly round the streets of Palma. After this, covered in blood and once more all but insensible, he was thrown back into his solitary chamber in the castle.

Only two nights after this appalling ordeal he was already casting round again how to make his escape. This time he found that the next-door room was some kind of butler's pantry containing piles of towels and napkins, services of plate and cutlery, and strings of puddings and sausages which he had not yet the appetite to eat. Knotting some towels together and using a table-knife to hack out a window bar, he climbed out through one of the upper windows and slid down the outside wall on the rope of towels, which, however, suddenly broke, depositing him in a well where he was nearly drowned. Recovering from this misadventure, he once again used the main drain to get him safely outside the city walls, and lay up for three days in the mountains.

Luckier than before, this time he came on a small boat lying under a tree in a private garden, got it down to the sea by night on some hand-cut wooden rollers, made a sail out of an old coat and a bit of his breeches, and pushed off, trusting himself boldly to the mercies of the wind and waves. The sea was very rough, but a north-easter carried him in less than two days onto the coast of North Africa. Turning his boat adrift, he walked ashore, weak with starvation but as he thought at last free, in the Gulf of Bougie, one hundred and twenty miles east of the city of Algiers, in the country of the fiercely xenophobic Kabyle Berbers.

Almost at once he fell in with a kindly old Moslem peasant who took him home, fried him a special wheat cake in butter –

the finest meal he had had in six years – and provided him
with a guide on the road to Algiers. But his troubles were by
no means over: long experience of Spanish adventurers
landing casually on their coast had made the Kabyles
suspicious of all unattached Europeans found wandering on
their territory. He also soon found the desire to turn him into a
Moslem as persistent in North Africa as the desire to turn him
into a Roman Catholic had been in Europe. Some slight
knowledge he had of ordnance, metalwork and joinery was
also at a premium, and lucrative offers were made to him by
the local potentates to stay and work for them as their official
artificer. All such offers he steadfastly refused, saying he
merely wished to get back to his wife and children in England;
so that he repeatedly found himself imprisoned again for
insubordination, repeatedly let out to superintend special jobs
(such as a *feu de joie* for a visiting sovereign or the construction
of a new waterworks), repeatedly using these periods of
freedom to escape and as repeatedly being recaptured and
thrown back into prison.

At last, having on one of these occasions taken to his heels in
a convenient thunderstorm and changed into an Arab outfit
he had stowed away against just such an opportunity, he
reached the city of Algiers; but here he suffered a crowning
piece of ill-luck in meeting by accident his old slave-master,
who having once paid for Hasleton's services did not see why
he should now dispense with them. Nor was the English
consul, to whom Hasleton had applied for an assisted passage
home, prepared to interfere with this state of affairs. Thus for
a whole further three years, eight voyages in all, Hasleton had
to serve once more as galley-slave, chained to an oar. It was
not till Christmas Eve 1592 that a friendly English merchant,
Richard Stapar, rescued him and brought him to London.
They arrived back in the *Cherubim* in February 1593.

3

A Long and Disconsolate Captivity

In spite of his name, Robert Knox came not from Scotland but from Suffolk; his father and grandfather were both born in the village of Nacton, down the Orwell estuary east of Ipswich, and there was that admixture of Dutch Huguenot blood in the family which so often seemed, and still seems, to fulfil itself in overseas adventure or some other kind of unconventional activity. The family was a seafaring one, and seamen must expect odd things to happen to them; but to spend nineteen of the best years of one's life, from 19 to 38, in a tropical climate under duress to a capricious and peculiar foreign tyrant, often himself hard pressed by his enemies, far exceeds what most seamen have to take in their stride.

The Knoxes, father and son, made their first voyage together from 1655 to 1657, to Fort St. George (Madras), Bengal and back to London. It paid well and they were in a hurry to leave again, in a new ship the *Ann*, for another venture; but meanwhile Cromwell had reorganised the ailing East India Company on a joint stock basis and given it a monopoly of eastern trade; so it was under this company's 1657 Charter that the Knoxes finally sailed on 21 January 1658. After some trading difficulties they ran into a storm off the south coast of India and had to take refuge in Kottiar Bay (better known today as Trincomalee) to repair their mast. While this was being done, Knox and his son and fourteen members of the crew were lured ashore by a manoeuvre of considerable ingenuity, forcibly detained, and taken into the 'long and disconsolate captivity' which for Robert Knox

Raja Singha the King of Ceylon

junior lasted nineteen years, but for his father only a few
months – Captain Robert Knox died of fever in his son's arms
in February 1661. The tamarind tree under which the
captivity negotiations took place was still shown to tourists up
to the last war.

The captivity was not, as captivities go, particularly
arduous: at all times the burden of feeding and housing the
internees, though not of clothing them, was laid as a formal
charge on the local villagers by royal decree. The fact is that
they had fallen into the hands of a ruler who had a
predilection for European foreigners and had collected a
whole menagerie of them, some 1,000 strong, spread here and
there over his dominions on this casual basis. Raja Singha II
(1610-1687) had succeeded his father as King of Kandy in
1635 and had at once been plunged into wars with the
Portuguese, whose occupation of Ceylon had not so far
penetrated into the central Kandyan uplands. He had early
turned to the Dutch for help in his struggles. Very few of the
foreigners who made their way to him to help or advise in this
continuous *va-et-vient* ever found their way home – he just liked
to keep them about the place, with their own consent if
possible, otherwise without. At one point he held five
successive Dutch ambassadors at court, none of them able to
escape, perhaps few of them willing; one of these ambassadors
having been sent up with the express purpose of securing the
release of the others.

It was known both to the East India Company and to the
Dutch that, in addition to his human zoo, Raja Singha liked to
collect animals, and various efforts were made to sway him by
this means; but the rigours of tropical travel in the
seventeenth century were such that few of these animal
offerings ever survived the journey. A Persian horse sent by the
Company in 1664 was intercepted by the Dutch and died at
sea; six 'lusty mastiffs' in 1667 had by two years later got only
as far as India where they all died; and a lion later reached the
island but never the monarch's presence. Hawks, tigers,
elephants and a large pond full of tame fish completed the
animal roll-call at court; at least one of the elephants being
trained as an executioner, apt to turn moody and truculent if

An Execution by an Elephant

deprived of its daily ration of criminals to maul and dismember.

Most of these European detainees, illustrious or otherwise, settled down in time, as they were officially encouraged to do, and married local wives – one of the *Ann*'s sailors, William Hubbard, returned to England only in 1706, after a fifty-year sojourn. Not so Robert Knox, whose energy and purposefulness were rooted deep, as these qualities often are, in puritanism and misogyny. The proper use of time is the basis of success, and Knox never wasted a moment: in the various villages where he found himself quartered he engaged in every enterprise open to him, from the knitting and sale of woollen caps at 9d. a time, via the ordinary occupations of a small-holder, fruit trees, goats, hens and hogs, up to the lending out of corn, which gave him a 50 per cent profit per annum. He had three different houses, the last of which, at Elladetta, 10 miles south of Kandy, he built with his own hands on land purchased with his own savings. In this he began to live about 1666 with three chosen bachelor friends, of whom two alas succumbed to the lure of matrimony, leaving him with the one faithful companion, Stephen Rutland, who stayed with him to the end.

Knox's upbringing at his mother's knee – his father being habitually at sea – had been one of exceptional piety and prayerfulness, so that religious thoughts were never out of his mind, and Bayly's *The Practice of Piety* never out of his pocket; he carried it into captivity with him. What was his joy then to learn, soon after his father's death, that an old villager had a tattered copy of the Bible for sale. Immediately he gathered together all his wealth – a single gold coin – and set off gladly to make the purchase; but no, said his servant, you need this money and I will get it for you for far less, if you will just behave to the old man as if you don't think much of it. In the end Knox gave one of his knitted caps in exchange for it, and all were delighted. It was his first lesson in buying and selling east of Suez.

Knox had been a whole twelve years in captivity before he was sent for personally by Raja Singha to present himself for interview. He stayed ten days at court in the new up-country capital of Digligy, in the hills above Kandy. (The massive, intricate and beautifully gold-plated throne of the Kandyan kings on which Raja Singha received Knox passed into the possession of the British in 1815 and was removed to Windsor Castle, where it was sometimes used for the Garter ceremony; but George V returned the throne to Ceylon in 1935, and Edward VIII the mace and remaining appurtenances during 1936, so that the whole is now reassembled and can be seen in the Colombo Museum. It would repay re-upholstery.) According to old Dutch prints of the period the throne was used under an elaborate canopy in an open throne room with crowds surging in and out, dogs barking, elephants watching, and much miscellaneous business being carried on all the while. In fact this particular confrontation was a short and inconclusive one, the Raja losing interest at once and waving his hand loftily for the matter to be arranged by a court official when he learnt that Knox had no desire to remain at court; and a few days later Knox sneaked off back home. He was sent for again, attended once more, slipped away again, and was thereafter left in peace at Elladetta.

From this point on he began to harden his plans for escape. He planned to set out with Stephen Rutland as travelling pedlars, to work their way to the north of the island in this guise and there give themselves up to the Dutch. The plan had the advantage of giving them a reason for travelling from place to place and being seen by military guards and the quite highly organised police system further and further afield on their usual peddling avocations, till at last they could come and go more or less as they wanted without attracting attention. The northern half of the island was, as it still is, the driest and least inhabited. They therefore accumulated a stock-in-trade of tobacco, pepper, garlic, combs and all sorts of iron ware, and set off on the preliminary journeys which would accustom the locals to their faces.

Their terror of offending the authorities, coupled with three or four years' drought on end, extended the period of these preliminary journeys to six or seven years, far longer than they had intended; and it was not till 22 September 1679 (exactly nineteen years after the Knoxes father and son had been

quartered together in their first village of Bandara Coswatta)
that the two fugitives felt it safe to set off on what they meant
to be their final journey of escape. Kindly entertained as
'innocent traders' by the Tamil governor of Anuradhapura –
conversation had to be by interpreter – they set out across the
jungle on 12 October, were terrified by nocturnal brushes with
elephants, alligators, a tiger and assorted wild men of the
woods, and finally came out to give themselves up to the
Dutch at Aripo Fort on 18 October. From here on it was
something of a triumphal progress via Manaar to Jaffna and
Colombo, in all of which places their appearance astonished
the local populace – bearded white men in Sinhalese clothes
with hair down to their waists – but they were freely and
merrily entertained by the Dutch. In Batavia, clothed and in
their right minds again, Stephen Rutland having recovered
from a crippling fever, they were closely questioned by the
Dutch governor, and treated as members of his family to some
unexpectedly high life. In the end they got back to London in
an English ship in September 1680, more than twenty-two
years after they had left.

On his return the East India Company voted Knox a
gratuity of £20, and Stephen Rutland £10, and encouraged
Knox to publish the bulky account of his adventures, the
composition of which, since he was never one to waste time,
had occupied his passage home from the East Indies. After
some editing by a clergyman cousin, and with a preface by Dr
Robert Hooke of the Royal Society (originally inaugurated as
the Royal Society of London for Improving Natural
Knowledge), *An Historical Relation of the Island of Ceylon, in the
East-Indies by Robert Knox, a Captive there near Twenty Years*,
appeared from the Royal Society's printer in 1681, and was
followed by German, Dutch and French editions in the next
decade. The British edition was instantly successful and was
much admired by Charles II, who gave the author an
audience.

It is a long, sprawling book, over 100,000 words, in four
parts: Part I a general description of the island, its flora, fauna
and agricultural practice; Part II an account of Raja Singha
II, his manners and system of government, his military

achievements and the abortive five-day rebellion against him in 1664; Part III of the inhabitants of the island, their religion, laws and customs: Part IV the story of Knox's own adventures, with notes on the other foreigners in the island. The unique particularity of detail, the engaging quaintness of the language, the sharpness with which the personality of the author stands out – nervous, inquisitive, mild, sympathetic to his captors, devout, but strangely terrified of women – combine to weld the whole into a memorable reading experience, quite apart from its historical value as the only dispassionate account of the Sri Lanka of its day. Here is a short sample, the general 'brief character' he gives the Sinhalese (or, as he writes it, 'Chingulays'):

> In short, in Carriage and Behaviour they are very grave and stately like unto the Portugals, in understanding quick and apprehensive, in design subtil and crafty, in discourse courteous but full of Flatteries, naturally inclined to temperance both in meat and drink, but not to Chastity, near and Provident in their Families, commending good Husbandry. In their dispositions not passionate, neither hard to be reconciled again when angry. In their Promises very unfaithful, approving lying in themselves, but misliking it in others; delighting in sloath, deferring labour till urgent necessity constrain them, neat in apparel, nice in eating; and not given to much sleep.

It is not a description with which those who know the modern Sinhalese could find much fault. And there are whole pages detailing farming practices which persist unchanged today.

The *Historical Relation* has a third importance in that it was known to Defoe, and is likely to have had some influence on the shaping of *Robinson Crusoe*, published in 1719. Defoe was a journalist whose knowledge of foreign parts was entirely book knowledge, supplemented by intelligent use of old Portuguese charts; and though it is easily possible to press the similarities too far, the later 'social' parts of *Crusoe*, when the hero has to deal with the arrival of new castaways on his island, do transcend what is known about the accepted original of the book, the solitary Alexander Selkirk, and may have been

The manner of their ploughing

based on Knox's experiences. Be that as it may, Defoe
certainly knew and admired Knox's book, of which he openly
includes a complete ten-page digest in a later novel *Captain
Singleton* (1720) 'so that the reader may value it as it deserves,
for the rarity as well as the truth of it'.

Still only forty when he got back to London, one of Knox's
first acts was to attend a 'mathematical schoole' to brush up
his navigation; and he then reported with his narrative to the
East India Company, which soon entrusted him with a new
ship in the China trade, the *Tonquin Merchant*, a command
which he held for thirteen years, making four voyages in her,
including slave trips to Madagascar and a call at Tristan da
Cunha, where a gale prevented his landing. In the course of
one of these voyages the *Tonquin Merchant* sprung a leak and
the decision was taken to enlarge her at the time of the repair;
this was done in the London dockyard by the drastic

CAPTAIN ROBERT KNOX
From the engraving by White in the Bodleian Library, Oxford

expedient of cutting the whole ship in half, adding an extra 12 feet (and 30 tons) amidships and splicing the whole together again. In 1697, in Cochin, S. India, Knox ran into Captain Blickland, a fellow captive of his from Ceylon – what celebrations they must have had.

More and more choosy and crotchety with old age, Knox turned down several lucrative shore jobs overseas offered him by the East India Company, including their chief factorship at Ispahan, and finally retired in 1701, settling in Wimbledon. To the last years of his life he left the ordering of various autobiographical notes and other writings which he left at his death to his nephew, and which did not reappear till they were discovered in the Bodleian in 1910. He died in 1720, still a bachelor, and was buried in Wimbledon church. Austere to the last, he left in his will £100 for funeral expenses, 'strictly forbidding all vaine gaudy cerimonies, and if any be left give it to Ye Poore without delay'. His great book is his memorial.

4

Young Drury

Only sixteen at the time of his shipwreck, Robert Drury owed his survival to his tender age, his white skin and fair hair, his curiosity value and a certain basic vitality which kept him going through a sequence of adventures which would certainly have overwhelmed a less high-spirited character. The son of a London publican (the King's Head in Old Jewry), he was born with a hankering for the sea which brooked no denial. Wishing to do his best for the boy, and hoping no doubt that the hardships of an actual voyage might put the nonsense out of his head for ever, his father fitted him out generously and entrusted him as passenger to Captain William Young, master of the *Degrave*, 700 tons, with fifty-two guns, bound for India. They left London in February 1701, and Robert never saw his father again.

All went well as far as Calcutta, where Robert taught himself to swim and acquired some knowledge of the habits of the common alligator which later stood him in excellent stead. They lost some forty of their crew through fever, including Captain Young himself, whose place was taken by his son, who had served till then as second mate. Going down the Hooghly on their way home, the *Degrave* went aground and sprang various leaks that kept them manning the pumps continuously all the way to Mauritius and thenceforward towards the Cape. By the time they were passing the south coast of Madagascar, the hold was half full of water and they took a collective decision to run the ship ashore, in spite of the advice of a member of the crew who claimed to know the area

round Fort Dauphine and warned them that the local king
was an enemy to all white men.

With the help of some fishermen on the beach, they were
lucky to get ashore through the boiling surf, which played
havoc with their fragile assortment of improvised rafts and
small boats and drowned three of their number. In all, about
one hundred and sixty were saved, including one woman and
a party of lascars who had been shipped in Mauritius to help
with the pumping. Among the last arrivals was Captain
Young, clutching in his hand the heart of his dead father,
destined for ultimate interment in England. A party of some
three hundred natives surrounded them on the beach and
began to make free with their possessions, anything made of
iron being specially prized. They provided some cattle to feed
the party, but shocked everyone by their drastic butchery
techniques. The saw being unknown to them, they hacked
straight through the animal, hide, flesh, bones and guts, and
roasted and ate the resulting cross-section as a whole. How
long, the nervous travellers wondered, before they are doing
the same to us?

It was not long. In fact at first the local king, before whom
they were haled, made it clear that he was delighted to have so
many visitors in his dominions, particularly if they would stay
and help him in his wars against his neighbours. He
mistrusted only the French, who precariously maintained a
small permanent settlement at Fort Dauphine, but had a
much higher opinion of the British with whom, as visiting
slave-traders, he had made many lucrative deals. Fearing
treachery all the time, however, the men of the party
embarked on a wild plan to kidnap the king and his son so as
to compel them to transport the whole party to the nearest
port. This succeeded for a while, but the ammunition
necessary to sustain such an operation soon ran out and the
natives chose a convenient moment during the journey to
massacre the whole party with great savagery and glee. Four
boys alone were saved, on account of their youth. Robert
Drury was one, destined as a slave for the king's grandson.

The society into which he found himself thus brutally
precipitated was something like that of the medieval Scottish

Highlands – small cattle-herd units, freebooting raids against neighbouring chiefs 'to murder and to ravish' and recurrent dynastic feuds. *Toake*, a powerful kind of honey mead, took the place of whisky, but life was cheap, wheeled vehicles were unknown and money did not exist. The guardian to whom Drury was assigned was a young man of capricious temper who, proud of his novel fair-skinned acquisition, treated him well in most respects and worked him hard, alternating between moments of spasmodic generosity and passionate rage if anything went wrong. In his first few years of slavery Drury several times came within an inch of getting himself speared through and through in the customary manner. Sometimes the ladies of the household, who had taken a great fancy to him, begged that he be spared; sometimes he was saved by a well-developed instinct of his own for getting the laugh on his side.

He was thought too valuable a possession to be taken on military expeditions with his guardian; but his position as major-domo in charge of the womenfolk and the vegetable garden became increasingly honourable. His duties included cultivating chick peas, yams and pulses, locating and developing wild honey supplies and, in particular, caring for his master's herds of half-tame humped beef cattle, these being then as they are today Madagascar's principal riches. A local superstition was that beef should be eaten only if killed by one of the blood royal; and his master, to save himself trouble, decided that Drury was of honourable enough descent to be preferred to the dignity of official butcher. All he had to do was to cut the throat, for others to carve the beast up; but in payment for this ceremonial service he quickly accumulated a small herd of his own. And all the while, the Malagasy being by nature a talkative, philosophical people, he improved his knowledge of their language and habits.

He discussed religion with them – tried, that is, to put over some of the story of Genesis he had learned at his mother's knee. Absurd, they said, a mere old wives' tale, this business about woman being made from a man's rib while he was asleep – if it were so, all men would be one rib short on one side, and they called forward a very thin man to demonstrate that this is not so. They pressed him hard to say whether Noah was a white or a black man, and could not understand why, if everything was destroyed in the Flood, God who made the creatures could not instantly make some more. He found his expositions hampered by the absence of any Malagasy phrase for 'above the heavens' and by the difficulty they found in visualising the Bible as a scriptural record, writing being totally unknown to them. Nevertheless, their enthusiasm and curiosity on these subjects were enormous: the same enthusiasm, perhaps, that made Madagascar so happy a field for the operations of the London Missionary Society in the following century, leading to the official conversion to Christianity of Queen Ranavalona II and her consort in 1869; the same curiosity, perhaps, that on this occasion inspired one of the local witch-doctors, who was found secretly boiling up a copy of the New Testament in his desperate desire to distil its singular power and bottle it for use as required.

Hunting was another sophisticated pastime the young men enjoyed. The wild cattle they went after fed at night and could be approached only after elaborate ablutions to clean all smell of smoke or sweat off the men's bodies. As they walked towards the grazing herd they would crop the tips of the tall grass with their hands to mimic a cow munching; and when they had at last got close enough to the animals in complete silence, they lanced them lightly – the kind of casual flesh wound another animal might make with its horns – and withdrew at once, to return by daylight to track the wounded animals by their blood trails. Judging the degree of wound to inflict was a matter of some delicacy, since lethal lancing would have caused the whole herd to run amok.

There was time for amorous dalliance too. The natives thought it unnatural for him to live without a wife, and allotted him a beautiful sixteen-year-old captured by chance with her family on a border raid. He fell very much in love with her modest, maidenly demeanour, though he set his face against having a child by her, fearing the jealous effect such an event might have on his guardian, and not wishing to enmesh himself in the ties of fatherhood.

For at no time did he allow either domestic bliss or his

growing personal prosperity to interfere with his determin-
ation to cut and run for home at an appropriate moment.
When he judged that the time had come – some two years
after his capture – saying good-bye to the girl was even harder
than keeping secret the preparation for the journey. He chose
to travel north-west to the port of St Augustine's Bay, which
was frequented by British slave-trading ships, rather than the
shorter distance north-east to Fort Dauphine under French
influence. It was an immensely arduous cross-country trek of
about one hundred and fifty miles, undertaken alone with the
minimum of baggage, and involving delays of months at a
time while he threw himself on the mercies of the various
chieftains whose territories he crossed and waited in their
company while they exhibited him proudly to their peoples
and discussed the outside world endlessly with him. On the
cross-country stages he lived on yams, dried beef and honey,
making do without fires as far as he could so as to evade any
pursuers there might be. One night, as he lay sleeping by his
dying camp-fire, he was set on by three wild foxes which, as
luck would have it, bit him first on the heel, not the throat,
and renewed their attack later. This incident caused him to lie
up for six days while he slowly reduced the swelling on his heel
with dressings of beef fat.

The first large river he came to was infested with alligators,
and, remembering from his time in Bengal that alligators hate
bright lights, he swam across it at night on his back, carrying
his spears in one hand and a blazing firebrand in the other.
Fortunately the night was still, and the brand remained alight
the whole way over. To negotiate the second, wider river, the
Onilahy, he had to improvise a rough kind of catamaran for
himself; and it was paddling this home-made craft that he
finally arrived within sight of St Augustine's Bay. Here he
made friends with an exiled Dutchman and various European
and West Indian outcasts, who must indeed have been
astonished at the sight of this fair-haired, freckled
Englishman, not yet twenty and all but naked, appearing
suddenly among them. The area, however, was very run down
and no ships appeared for many months; instead a marauding
expedition from farther north entered the district, and soon

Drury found himself once more captured and sold into slavery.

Several years passed before he had the chance to journey still farther north up the coast into the Sakalava country, which he knew to be the centre from which the sturdiest slaves, those of black African stock, were regularly shipped to the West Indies. His fortunes rose and fell. He found himself treated like royalty, then sold into slavery, periodically racked with fevers and the yaws, and pressed into joining freebooting expeditions in which he had no interest and which caused him to miss at least two passing ships that might have taken him home.

At one point in those years, seeing an English ship in Morondava Bay, he sent down to the captain by native runner a letter rolled in a palmetto leaf. This leaf the runner lost on the way and replaced with another of his own gathering, so that the captain threw it away, not understanding what it was all about, and the runner reported accordingly to Drury on his return. It was the most agonising disappointment in his whole story; but though the ship sailed without him, it did happen to take on board another English exile who was later able, more or less by chance, to get in touch with Drury's father in London.

Drury was finally befriended, in the up-country Sakalava capital, Mohabo, by a crippled chieftain of a civilised and philosophical turn of mind, with whom he lived in some state for at least two and a half years, and who was so taken by his white companion that he made it very difficult for Drury to leave when eventually the right ship did arrive, bearing a letter for him from his father. Captain Mackett, in charge of the slave ship, turned the scale at last by offering a ransom payment of a new gun with powder, flints and a case of spirits. He then took Drury on board, shaved off his matted hair and fitted him out in seaman's white drill – so that after fifteen years he was respectable again at last. After some months spent loading slaves up and down the coast, they left on 20th January 1717 via St Helena and Barbados, where the slaves were unshipped, and were back in London in September. Drury found that his father had died about a year before, leaving him £200.

Scarcely surprising, perhaps, that after so many ups and downs Drury found it impossible to settle in any kind of shore job, and decided to take service a year later with a friend of

Captain Mackett's in the *Mercury*, on another slave-buying voyage to Madagascar. They spent six months on the island, during which Drury met many old friends and turned his knowledge of the language to excellent use as interpreter. They were back again in London two years later, after delivering their cargo in the West Indies and America.

Of the rest of his life little is known. He lived in Lincoln's Inn Fields, had a job as porter with the East India Company, and on fine summer evenings liked to demonstrate to his friends and others a few feats of dexterity with a spear he had picked up in Madagascar. The date and place of his death are not known.

5

The *Wager*

The *Wager* must be one of the best documented in the whole long line of British shipwrecks. It is not merely that four separate narratives exist of the survivors' adventures getting home; but there is a fascination in the whole long arc of the story, which begins with a premonition of disaster, issued by an ex-captain of the ship who knew what he was talking about, and ends six years later with a decision of their lords of the Admiralty on a nice point of naval law. Wager Island, Byron Island and Anna Pink Bay are still to be found in modern maps of the coast of Chile, incongruously assorted with the Esmeraldas, Magdalenas and other names of Spanish provenance. (To keep at hand the largest available map of the southern end of South America will add greatly to an understanding of the *Wager* story; the jagged, tortured disorder of the islands, bays, straits and headlands strewn along the coast exactly symbolises the roughness of the life the survivors led.)

The *Wager* was an old East India merchantman converted and armed for use as a storeship in support of a punitive expedition led by Captain George Anson in 1740 against the Spaniards in Chilean waters. Its unwieldy size and tub-like qualities were responsible both for its falling behind the rest of the fleet, so that it was wrecked on its own out of touch with the others; and for its being able to supply its marooned crew for longer than a more seaworthy ordinary ship might have done. Even though only a part of the cargo could be salvaged – and the alcohols brought ashore permitted an issue of one pint

J. Wale delin.   C. Grignion s.

The Wreck of the *Wager*

of brandy per man per day for some time – it is doubtful if so many of the ship's complement would have survived at all on these inhospitable shores, if they had had to rely on the stores content of a smaller vessel. Limpets, armadillos, wild celery, dogs, boiled seaweed and rotting seal meat supplemented a dwindling diet which brought them close to cannibalism at times; but resourceful use was made, not only of the stores, but also of the muskets, ammunition, bales of cloth and miscellaneous containers rescued from the wreck. Even so, such was the confusion, so vile the weather and so prevalent the inertia caused by food-poisoning that it was eleven days before a store tent could be organised, from which provisions could be dispensed on something like a regular basis. The *Wager* carried a small complement of marines, who must not, however, be thought of as the highly trained and disciplined marines of today; they seem to have been press-ganged at the last minute from the Royal Hospital, Chelsea, and to have had little taste for seagoing apart from the prospect, which animated all of them, of returning home one day as part owners of a prize ship, or other maritime loot.

After the *Wager* had been blown, on the night of 14 May 1741, onto a lee shore in Patagonia and broken its back on the rocks, two schools of thought arose among the survivors about what to do next. The first, led by the master gunner John Bulkeley and the ship's carpenter John Cummins, was for returning slowly south-eastwards in the ship's longboat through the Straits of Magellan round to the River Plate, where they expected to be able to take ship for Europe. The second, led by Captain Cheap, was for carrying on up the coast; Cheap, who combined obstinacy with a capacity for self-delusion and a hot temper, held that it was still his duty to pursue the Spanish foe according to his orders, board one of their ships and bring it home as a prize. It is the parallel accounts of these two main parties travelling in different directions, that are the backbone of the *Wager* story.

Of the two accounts that of John Bulkeley has superior actuality and vividness from being written day by day as he went along, starting each day with the matter of greatest moment to a seaman, the weather, and supported, since he was a bit of a sea-lawyer, by occasional signed manifestos from his fellow shipmates. The Hon. John Byron's account of the Cheap party's misfortunes is recollected in tranquillity twenty years later, after he had risen to the rank of admiral and was thinking back to events which had occurred to him when he was a seventeen-year-old midshipman. (John Byron was the grandfather of Lord Byron, author of *Don Juan* – who wrote of him 'He had no peace at sea, nor I on land'.)

Speaking mathematically, John Bulkeley's venture must be accounted more successful than Captain Cheap's: out of the seventy who left Wager Island with Bulkeley thirty reached the River Plate, while out of the twenty who stayed with Cheap only four, including Byron, reached the safety of Chiloe Island further up the coast – where of course, so far from boarding a Spanish vessel, they were almost too weak to stand and were soon handed over to the Spanish as prisoners of war. In the end they were transferred from Chiloe to Valparaiso, thence 90 miles up country to the capital Santiago, where they spent two years, then back to the coast and ultimately home across the Atlantic in a French frigate.

All accounts pay tribute to the exceptional technical skill of the ship's carpenter, John Cummins, who succeeded, with the scratch labour, tools and timber available to him, working for most of the time in mist or blinding rain, in cutting the *Wager*'s longboat in half and adding an extra twelve feet to its length, and improvising a soap-and-tallow caulking for the result, so that it successfully withstood a coastal voyage of more than 1,000 miles in those infernally tricky waters. Perhaps John Cummins should be regarded as the true hero of the story.

The third of the four accounts available to us is that of a midshipman, Alexander Campbell who travelled with the Cheap party as far as Santiago, and there in January 1745 detached himself to join – presumably in the role of a prisoner on parole – a group of four Spanish naval officers walking eastwards across the Andes, a thirsty seven-week slog, to Buenos Aires. Here Campbell was reunited with the writer of the fourth *Wager* story, Isaac Morris, another midshipman, who had led a party of eight on foot all the way round the

coast of Patagonia. This hazardous course had been forced on
him by the treachery of some other members of a *Wager*
foraging party who, after filling their boat, rowed off without a
word, leaving Morris and seven others stranded on shore.
During their long, wintry walk round the coast they had lived
mainly on the meat of seals and armadillos which they killed
with clubs or stones. After some months in the hands of
Indians who treated them all the better when they heard that
England was at war with the hated Spaniards, they finally
made Buenos Aires, where the Spanish provincial governor
paid the Indians a ransom of 90 dollars for the whole party
and then put them as prisoners on board a man-of-war lying
in the river. From this Morris escaped and swam ashore, but
being recaptured was put in the stocks 'neck and heels' four
hours every day for a fortnight. In October 1745 they sailed for
Spain, survived a crew mutiny on board, were thrown into
prison again and finally, through the good offices of the British
consul in Lisbon, got home in April 1746. The party was
reduced to three in number.

For all four parties communication had been a major
difficulty throughout. Apart from the occasional exchange of
ideas in dog Latin with a Jesuit, a word or two of Spanish was
all that anyone could manage, and no words at all of the
speech of the various native tribes with whom they had to
deal. With these sign language or plain brute force was the
order of the day. On a foraging party one of the starving
Englishmen had assembled a lot of limpets in his hat and in
the boat on the way home was beginning to eat them
voraciously, hurling the shells over his shoulder into the sea;
the Indians ferrying him immediately fell on him in silence
and half-strangled him – it was apparently their ritual custom
to dump all limpet shells back on shore after consumption.

They were constantly kept guessing too by the Spaniards,
whose conduct oscillated between the utmost military severity
and the utmost in hospitality and kindness, including
generous dowry offers from the mothers of marriageable
daughters if the Englishmen (or at least the more handsome of
them) would stay and settle in Patagonia. And there were
endless religious discussions by interpreter with Jesuit priests

seeking (not always in vain) to persuade them over to Rome from their English Protestant convictions. It was therefore something of a relief to reach Buenos Aires, where some of the English residents, particularly a Mr Grey, took them in charge, lent them money and clothes and helped them on their way to Europe.

Several years later, after all concerned, including Captain Cheap, had reached England again by various routes, Bulkeley had to face an official enquiry whether his action had constituted mutiny. Their lordships of the Admiralty ruled in the end, after consulting the commodore of the expedition Captain Anson, that since the *Wager* had broken up on the rocks, it no longer existed, so that Cheap could no longer be regarded as its captain, so that mutiny against his authority was not possible: 'there had been errors and misdemeanours on both sides.' (Modern naval ratings should perhaps not be too confident that their lordships would take a similar view of similar conduct after a shipwreck today!)

Countless memorable incidents will reward those who have leisure to embark on further study of these *Wager* records: a picture of the men sitting huddled together all night along the longboat's gunwale so as to minimize with their row of serried backs the force of the mountainous waves breaking into their boat; their strange superstitions about burying their dead comrades; Indians, puzzled by a hand mirror, trying to get round to the back of it and find the owner of the face they saw in it; an elephant seal chewing up a rifle and bayonet as if they were matchwood; the extra comfort that the petty officers, like petty officers all the world over, contrived to introduce into their hut at the end of nowhere; and so on. There should be a special salute too for the tough old cook Thomas Maclean, who even at the age of 82 outlasted so many of his fellows, and indeed finally succumbed to starvation only two days before the Bulkeley party unexpectedly reached civilisation again on the Rio Grande. All in all, however, it is the grand sweep of the whole that gives it its compelling interest, especially to connoisseurs of extreme situations; the interactions between civilised and uncivilised people (and those adjectives have nothing to do with the colour of anyone's skin); the probing of the essence of leadership and command, and of the deeply ingrained social stratifications of the English.

There are decisions to take too, as Byron had to take them: after weeks in the paralysing agonies of extreme hunger, is it better to eat your sealskin shoes (raw) or to continue eating nothing at all?

6

Four Russians on Spitzbergen

In the year 1743, Jeremiah Okladmkof, a merchant of Mesen, in the province of Jugovia, and government of Archangel, in Russia, fitted out a vessel for the Greenland whale-fishery. She carried fourteen men, and was destined for Spitzbergen. For eight successive days after their sailing the wind was fair, but on the ninth it changed; so that instead of getting to the coast of Spitzbergen, the usual rendezvous of the Dutch ships, they were driven eastward, and after some days elapsed they found themselves near an island, called by the Russians Little Broun. Approaching within three versts, or two English miles of this island, the vessel was suddenly surrounded by ice, and the crew were reduced to an extremely dangerous situation.

In this alarming state, a council was held, when the mate, Alexis Himkof, informed his comrades that some of the people of Mesen formerly intended wintering on this island, and for that purpose had carried timber hither, fit for building a hut, and actually erected one at some distance from the shore.

The whole crew, therefore, concluded to winter there, if the hut, as they hoped, still existed, because they were exposed to imminent danger by remaining in the ship; and they would infallibly perish if they did so. Four of the crew were, on that account, dispatched in search of it, or of any other assistance they might meet with.

The names of these four were, Alexis Himkof, Iwan Himkof, Stephen Scharapof and Feodor Weregin. Two miles of ice intervened between them and the shore, which being loose, and driven together by the wind, rendered the approach

47

difficult and dangerous. Providing themselves with a musket, a powder-horn containing twelve charges of powder, with as many balls, an axe, a kettle, about twenty pounds of flour, a knife, a tinder-box, some tobacco, and each his wooden pipe, they soon arrived on the island.

Their first employment was exploring the country, when they discovered the hut alluded to, about a mile and a half from the shore. It was thirty-six feet long, eighteen broad, and eighteen high; and consisted of two chambers. Rejoicing greatly at their success, they passed the night in it, though having been built a considerable time, it had suffered much from the weather.

Next morning the four men hastened to the shore, impatient to communicate their good fortune to their comrades; likewise designing to get such stores, ammunition, and necessaries from the vessel, as to enable them to winter on the island. But the reader may conceive their sorrow and astonishment, when on reaching the place where they had landed, nothing was to be seen but an open sea, instead of the ice, which only the day preceding had covered it. Doubtless a violent storm, which arose during the night, had operated the change. It was not known, however, whether the vessel had been beat to pieces by the ice, or whether she had been carried by the current to the ocean; not an uncommon event in Greenland. Whatever accident befell her, certain it is they saw her no more; whence it is probable that she sunk, and that all on board perished.

This unfortunate occurrence deprived them of the hope of ever being able to quit the island, and full of horror and despair, they returned to the hut. But their first attention was directed to the means of providing subsistence, and repairing their habitation. The twelve charges of powder procured them as many reindeer, for the island, fortunately for them, abounded with these animals.

Though there were many crevices in the building, the wood of the hut was still sound and unimpaired, therefore the deficiency was supplied and done the more easily, because the lower class of Russians are expert carpenters. Here they had plenty of moss to assist them.

The intense cold of the climate prevents the growth of

vegetables, and no species of tree or shrub is found on the Islands of Spitzbergen. The Russians, however, collected a quantity of wood on the shore, which at first consisted of the wrecks of vessels, and afterwards of whole trees with their roots, the produce of some more hospitable climate, though unknown. Fortunately they found several bits of old iron, some nails, five or six inches long, and an iron hook, on a few wooden boards washed in by the sea. They likewise found the root of a fir-tree bent and nearly fashioned into the shape of a bow.

By the help of a knife, a bow was soon formed, but wanting a string and arrows. Unable at present to procure either, they resolved to make two lances to defend themselves against the white bears. The iron hook was therefore fashioned into a hammer, by widening a hole which it happened to have about the middle, with one of the largest nails. A large pebble served for an anvil, and a couple of reindeer horns served for the tongs.

By means of such tools, two spear heads were made, which were tied fast with thongs to sticks about the thickness of a man's arm. Thus equipped, the Russians ventured to attack a white bear, and, after a most dangerous encounter, succeeded in killing it. This was a new supply of provisions: they relished the flesh exceedingly, and easily divided the tendons into filaments, which, besides other uses, served for strings to their bow.

The Russians, in the next place, proceeded to forge some bits of iron into smaller pieces, resembling the head of the spears, and these were fitted to arrows, by fastening them to fir rods. They had thus a complete bow and arrows, and were more easily enabled to obtain food. With these, during their abode on the island, they killed no less than two hundred and fifty reindeer, and a great number of blue and white foxes. They fed on the flesh of the animals, and used their skins for clothing. They killed only ten white bears during their residence, and that at the utmost hazard, for these creatures are amazingly strong, and defended themselves with surprising vigour and fury. The first was attacked intentionally; the other nine were killed in self-defence, for the animals even ventured to enter the outer room of the hut to devour them. Some, less ferocious than others, were repulsed on the first attempt, but a repetition of their attacks exposed the sailors to the continual apprehension of being destroyed.

As they could not afford wood for a constant fire, they dried a portion of their provision in the open air, and afterwards hung it up in the hut, which was always full of smoke. Prepared in this way, they used it for bread, because they were under the necessity of eating their other flesh half raw.

Unfortunately, one of the Russians was attacked by the scurvy. Iwan Himkof, who had wintered several times on the coast of West Spitzbergen, advised his companions to swallow raw and frozen meat in small pieces; to drink the blood of the reindeer, as it flowed warm from the veins of the animal, and to eat scurvy-grass, although it was not very abundant. Those who followed his injunctions found an effectual antidote, but Feodor Weregin, being naturally of an indolent disposition, averse to drinking the reindeer blood, and, unwilling to leave the hut when he could possibly avoid it, was soon seized with the scurvy. Under this afflicting distemper he passed nearly six years, enduring the greatest sufferings. At length he became so weak that he could not sit erect, nor even raise his hand to his mouth, so that his humane companions were obliged to attend on, and feed him like a new born infant until the hour of his death.

In the course of their excursions through the island, the seamen had met with a slimy loam, or kind of clay, of which they contrived to make a lamp, and proposed to keep it constantly burning with the fat of the animals they should kill. Thus they filled it with reindeer's fat, and stuck a bit of twisted linen into it for a wick. But, to their mortification, always as the fat melted, it not only was absorbed by the clay, but fairly ran through it on all sides. On this account they formed another lamp, which they dried thoroughly in the air, and heated red hot. It was next quenched in their kettle, wherein they had boiled a quantity of flour down to the consistence of thin starch. When filled with melted fat, they found, to their great joy, that it did not leak. Encouraged by this attempt, they made another, so that, at all events, they might not be destitute of light, and saved the remainder of their flour for similar purposes. Oakum thrown ashore, as also cordage found among the wrecks of vessels, served for wicks; and when these resources failed, they converted their shirts and drawers to the same purpose. By such means they kept a lamp burning from soon after their arrival on the island, until the day of their embarkation for their native country.

Clothes, in so rigorous a climate, next became an object of necessity. The uses to which they had applied what they had brought with them exposed them still more to its severity. The skins of reindeer and foxes had hitherto served for bedding. It was essential to devise some method of tanning them, the better to withstand the weather. This was accomplished, in a certain degree, by soaking the skins in water until the hair could be rubbed off, and then putting reindeer fat upon them. The leather, by such a process, became soft and pliant. The want of awls and needles was supplied by bits of iron occasionally collected: of these they made a kind of wire, which, being heated red hot, was pierced with a knife, ground to a sharp point, which formed the eye of a needle. The sinews of bears and reindeer, split into threads, served for sewing the pieces of leather together, which enabled the Russians to procure jackets and trousers for summer dress, and a long fur gown with a hood for their winter apparel.

The wants of these unfortunate persons being thus provided for, the only reflections disturbing them were regret for those left behind at home, or the apprehension of some one of them surviving all his companions, and then either famishing for want of food, or becoming a prey to wild beasts. The mate, Alexis Himkof, had a wife and three children, who were constantly in his mind, and he was unhappy from the dread of never seeing them more.

Excepting white bears, foxes, and reindeer, with which the island abounds, no other animals inhabit it. A few birds are seen in summer, such as geese, ducks, and other water-fowl. Whales seldom approach the shore; but there are great numbers of seals: other fish are scarce; and indeed their being in plenty would have little availed the Russians, who were unprovided with the means of taking them. Sometimes they found the teeth and jaws of seals on the shore, but never an entire carcase; for when these animals die on land, the white bears immediately eat them. The common food of this ferocious creature, however, is the flesh of dead whales, which are frequently seen floating about in the polar regions, and are sometimes cast on shore. When this provision fails, they fall upon seals, devouring these and other animals sleeping on the beach.

The island had many mountains and steep rocks of stupendous height, perpetually covered with snow and ice: not a tree, nor even the poorest shrub was to be met with;: neither is there any vegetable but scurvy-grass, though plenty of moss grows in every part. The Russians found no river; however, there were many small rivulets rising among the rocks and mountains, which afforded a quantity of water.

They saw the sun moving for months together round the horizon during summer, and in winter they were an equal length of time in total darkness; but the Aurora Borealis, which was then frequent, contributed to lessen the gloominess of so long a night. Thick cloudy weather, great quantities of snow, and almost incessant rain at certain seasons, often obscured the stars. The snow totally covered the hut in winter, and left them no way of getting out of it, excepting by a hole which they had made in the roof of one of the chambers.

When the unfortunate mariners had passed nearly six years in this dismal abode, Feodor Weregin, who had all along been in a languid state, died; after suffering the most excruciating pains. Though his companions were thus freed of the trouble of attending on him, and the grief of witnessing his misery, they were deeply affected by his death. They saw their number lessened, and each wished to be the next to follow him. Having died in winter, a grave as deep as possible was dug in the snow to receive his corpse, and the survivors then covered it over to the best of their power, to prevent the white bears from getting at it.

While the melancholy reflections excited by Weregin's death were still fresh in the minds of his comrades, and while each expected to pay the like duties to the companions of his misfortunes that they had done to him, or to be himself the first to receive them, a Russian vessel unexpectedly came in view on 15 August 1749.

This vessel belonged to a trader who had come to Archangel, and intended to winter in Nova Zembla: but fortunately it was proposed to him to winter at West Spitzbergen, to which, after many objections, he assented. Contrary winds on the passage prevented the ship from reaching the place of her destination, and drove her towards East Spitzbergen, directly opposite to the residence of the mariners. As soon as they perceived her, they hastened to light fires on the nearest hills, and then ran to the beach waving a flag made of a reindeer's skin fastened to a pole. The people on board observing these signals, concluded there were men ashore imploring their assistance, and therefore came to an anchor near the island.

To describe the joy of the unfortunate mariners at seeing the moment of their deliverance so near is impossible. They soon agreed with the master of the vessel to take them and all their riches on board, for which they should work during the voyage, and pay him eighty rubles on arriving in Russia. Therefore they embarked, carrying with them two thousand weight of reindeer fat, many hides of the same animals, the skins of the blue and white foxes and bears they had killed. Neither did they neglect to carry away their spears, their knife and axe, which were almost worn out, or their awls and needles, which were carefully preserved in a box, very ingeniously made of bone.

After spending six years and three months in this rueful solitude, they arrived safe at Archangel on 25 September 1749. But the moment of landing was nearly fatal to the affectionate wife of Alexis Himkof, who happened to be present when the vessel came into port. Immediately recognising her husband, she ran with such eagerness to embrace him, that she slipped into the water, and very narrowly escaped being drowned.

All the three survivors were strong and healthy: having lived so long without bread, they could not be reconciled to the use of it; neither could they bear spirituous liquors, and drank nothing but water.

As they were vassals of Count Schuwalow, who then had a

grant of the whale fishery, M. Le Roy requested of him that they might be sent from Archangel to St Petersburgh, where he could satisfy himself respecting their adventures. Accordingly two of them arrived, Alexis Himkof, aged about fifty, and Iwan Himkof, about thirty. They brought some curious specimens of their workmanship, so neatly executed that it was doubtful with what tools it could have been done. From their account, both to M. Klingstadt, auditor of the Admiralty at Archangel, and what they now communicated, M. Le Roy composed the preceding narrative.

The place where the preceding events occurred is not altogether evident, for it is not clearly explained what country in particular is to be understood by *East Spitzbergen*, whether the extensive tract known by the specific name of Spitzbergen, or any island in the vicinity. Most probably, however, from the animals described, the scene of the misfortunes of the Russians lay in Spitzbergen, properly so called.

The northern part of that country, so far as hitherto explored, reaches beyond 81° of north latitude, and extends to between 76 and 77° south. But whether it forms an island, or is united to the continent of America, is questioned by navigators and geographers.

For centuries past it has been greatly resorted to on account of the profitable whale-fishery of the surrounding seas, and several shipwrecks, as well as incidents similar to the preceding, have occurred there, and in the vicinity. Spitzbergen is a bleak and barren country, and received its name from the lofty pointed mountains by which it is covered: perpetual snow prevails, few plants spring from the soil, and it is destitute of wood. But to compensate in some measure for the scanty productions of nature by land, its seas, abundantly stored with fish, can afford a copious supply both of food and clothing to mankind.

7

Trading with the Natives

The *Doddington*, Captain Samson, sailed from the Downs, 23 April 1755, in company with the *Pelham*, the *Houghton*, the *Streatham*, and the *Edgecourt*, all in the service of the East India Company. In about seven days they cleared the Channel, during which time Captain Samson perceived that his ship sailed faster than any of the others. Unwilling to lose the benefit of this superiority, by keeping company with the rest, he stood on alone, and soon lost sight of them. On 20 May, he made Bonavista, one of the Cape de Verd Islands, in 16° of north latitude, and on the 21st got into Porto Pryor (Praya) Bay. It now appeared that he had either been mistaken in supposing his ship to outsail the rest of the fleet, or that he had lost time by the course he had steered, for the *Pelham* and the *Streatham*, he found, had reached the bay two days before him. The *Houghton* arrived soon afterwards, but the *Edgecourt* did not come in till the 26th.

On the 27th the *Doddington*, *Pelham*, *Streatham*, and *Houghton*, having taken in their water, proceeded on the voyage together, leaving the *Edgecourt* in the road. They continued in company until the 28th, when Captain Samson thinking the course too far easterly, ordered the *Doddington* to be kept south, which again separated her from the rest of the fleet; and after a fine voyage of seven weeks, she made the land of the Cape of Good Hope.

A new departure was taken from Cape Needles, on July, just after doubling the Cape of Good Hope, and the vessel having steered eastward about twenty-four hours, between

latitude 35° 30' and 36°, the captain ordered her to be kept
east-north-east. In this course she continued until about a
quarter before one in the morning until about a quarter before
one in the morning of Thursday, 17 July, when she struck.

The officer, whose journal afforded the materials for this
narrative, was then asleep in his cabin, but being suddenly
awakened by the shock, he started up in the utmost
consternation, and hastened on deck. Here all the terrors of
his situation at once rushed on him. He saw the men dashed to
and fro by the violence of the sea rolling over them, and the
ship breaking to pieces at every stroke of the surge. Crawling
over to the larboard of the quarter-deck, which lay highest out
of the water, he there found the captain, who said very little
more than that all must perish. In a few minutes a sea parted
them, and he saw him no more. He made a shift to get back to
the quarter-deck, though very much bruised, and with the
small bone of his left arm broken. All the rest of the ship was
then under water, and shattered to pieces.

In this dreadful situation, expecting every moment to be
swallowed up, he heard somebody cry out *land!* He looked
eagerly about him, but notwithstanding he saw something,
which he supposed was taken for land, he believed it was only
the surge of the sea on the other side of the breakers. At the
same moment the sea broke over him with great violence, and
not only forced him from his hold, but stunned him by a
violent blow on the eye.

Though from this time he lay insensible till after day-light,
he still continued on the wreck; and when he recovered, he
found himself fixed to a plank, by a nail that had been forced
into his shoulder. Besides the pain of his wounds and bruises,
he now felt himself so benumbed with cold, that he could
scarce move either hand or foot. He called out as loud as he
could to the people on the rocks, but they were unable to give
him any assistance, whence a considerable time elapsed before
he was capable of disengaging himself and crawling ashore.

This shore was a barren uninhabited rock in 33° 44' south
latitude, and distant about 250 leagues east of the Cape of
Good Hope. Here were now met Mr Evan Jones, chief-mate;
Mr John Cottes, Mr William Webb, and Mr S. Powell,

second, third, and fifth mates; Richard Topping, carpenter; Neil Bothwell, and Nathaniel Chisholm, quarter-masters; Daniel Ladova, captain's steward; Henry Sharp, the surgeon's servant; Thomas Arnold, a black, and John M'Dowal, servants to the captain; Robert Beaseley, John Ding, Gilbert Cain, Terence Mole, Jonas Rosenbury, John Glass, —— Taylor, and Hendrick Scantz, seamen; John Yets, midshipman; John Lister, Ralph Smith, and Edward Dysoy, matrosses. These persons, being twenty-three in number, were the whole surviving of 270 souls that were on board when the ship struck.

Their first care was to search for some covering among the things thrown on the rocks from the ship, in which they succeeded beyond expectation. The next article of necessity which they felt the want of, was fire, which was not so easily supplied. Some of their number made an unsuccessful attempt to kindle two pieces of wood, by rubbing them together; others went prying about the rocks, to pick up something that might serve for a flint and steel. After long search, they found a box containing two gun flints and a broken file. This was a joyful acquisition, though they were still destitute of any thing that would kindle from a spark; and until a substitute for tinder could be procured, the flint and steel were useless. A further search was therefore undertaken, with inexpressible solicitude and anxiety, and at last a cask of gunpowder was discovered, which, however, to their great disappointment, proved to be wet: but on a more narrow inspection, a small quantity that had suffered no damage was found at the bottom of the cask. Some of this they bruised on a linen rag, and it served them very well for tinder.

A fire was soon made, around which the bruised and wounded collected, and the rest went in quest of other necessaries, without which the rock could afford them but a very short respite from destruction. In the afternoon, a box of wax-candles, and a case of brandy, were brought in. Both were extremely acceptable, particularly the latter, of which each individual deemed it advisable to take a dram. Some others of the party returned soon after, with an account of their having discovered a cask almost full of fresh water, which was of still greater consequence than the spirits. Mr Jones brought in several pieces of salt pork, and others arrived, driving seven hogs before them, which had come on shore alive. Casks of beer, water, and flour, were also seen at a distance, but it was not then possible to get them over the rocks.

Night approaching, rendered it necessary to provide some shelter; all hands were therefore employed in making a tent of some canvas cast ashore, but the quantity recovered was so small, that the tent could not hold them all. For fear of being overflowed, they were obliged to erect it on the highest part of the island, which was covered with the dung of a water-fowl, rather larger than a gannet, that much frequented it. Those unable to walk were placed under the tent, and a fire kindled near them. They had passed the day without food, and were now deprived of rest during the night, for, independent of being sunk a foot in the dung, the wind was so tempestuous, that it scattered about their fire, and, before it could be again collected, the rain put it out. In the morning, those who were able went again in search of what could be saved from the wreck; but, to their great mortification, they found all the casks which were seen the preceding night, except one of flour and another of beer, staved against the rocks. These, however, they secured, and soon after, the tide flowing up, interrupted their operations. The company were, therefore, called together to eat their first meal, and some pork was broiled on the coals for dinner.

Sitting down, thus desolate and forlorn, to a repast which they were wont to share in the convivial cheerfulness which the consciousness of plenty inspired, struck them with such a sense of their present condition, that they burst into passionate exclamations, wringing their hands, and looking around with all the wildness of despair. Amidst such tumultuous emotions, our reflections hurry from one subject to another, in quest of something from which comfort may be derived: And here one of the survivors, recollecting that the carpenter was among them, and that he might build a strong sloop, providing he could obtain tools and materials, suggested it as a ground of hope to the rest. Every one's attention was immediately directed towards the carpenter, who declared his belief that, providing tools and materials could be found, he should be able to build a sloop that would carry them all to a port of safety. At that time, indeed, they entertained no prospect of procuring either, nor of being able to victual such a vessel, had they even had it ready built. Yet, no sooner had they wrested their deliverance one remove beyond total impossibility, than they seemed to think it neither improbable nor difficult; they began to eat without repining: that moment the boat engrossed their whole conversation, and they not only debated on her size and rigging, but to what port they should steer, whether to the Cape or Delagoa.

As soon as the repast was finished, some went to mend the tent, and others in search of tools, but none were found that day.

On Saturday the 19th, four butts of water were secured, one cask of flour, one hogshead of brandy, and a small boat, which had been thrown up by the tide, in a shattered condition. Still no tools were found except a scraper. But next day they had the good fortune to discover a hamper containing files, sail-needles, gimblets, and an azimuth compass card. They also found two quadrants, a carpenter's adze, a chisel, three sword blades, and a chest of treasure. As a prodigious surf had been rolling in all the day before, which it was reasonably expected would throw something up, the search was made early in the morning. At ten o'clock all assembled to prayers; and, not going out again until after dinner, they then found most of the packets belonging to the king and the company, which they carefully dried and laid aside.

While searching about the beach, they found the body of a lady, which they recognized to be that of Mrs Collet, the wife of the second mate, who was himself then at a little distance. The mutual affection subsisting between this couple was of remarkable tenderness; and Mr Jones, the first mate, immediately stepped to Mr Collet, and contrived to take him to the other side of the rock, while the other two mates, the carpenter, and some others, dug a grave, where they deposited the body, reading the funeral service over it, from a French prayer-book, which had driven ashore from the wreck along with the deceased.

Having thus paid the last tribute to one of their unfortunate number, and concealed from Mr Collet a sight which would have most sensibly, if not fatally, affected him, some days afterwards they found means gradually to disclose what they had done, and to restore him the wedding-ring, which they had taken from her finger. He received it with great emotion, and in future spent many days in raising a monument over the grave, by piling up the squarest stones he could find, and fixing an elm plank on the top, inscribed with her name, her age, and the time of her death, and also some account of the fatal accident by which it was occasioned.

On Monday 21 July, more water and pork, as likewise some timber, plank, cordage, and canvas, were recovered. These the survivors joyfully secured for the projected boat, though yet in want of many implements indispensable for the carpenter proceeding with his work. He had just finished a saw, though he had neither hammer nor nails. It happened, however, that one of the seamen, Hendrick Scantz, a Swede, having picked up an old pair of bellows, brought them to his companions, telling them that he had been a smith by profession, and that with these bellows and a forge, which he hoped by his direction they should be able to build, he could furnish the carpenter with all necessary tools, nails included, as plenty of iron might be obtained by burning it out of the timber of the wreck coming ashore. This account was received with a transport of joy; the smith immediately set himself to mend the bellows; and the three following days were occupied in building a tent and forge, and in collecting the timber and plank for the carpenter's use, who also was employed in preparing the few tools already in his possession, that the boat might be begun as soon as possible.

On Thursday 24 July, the carpenter, assisted by Chisholm the quarter-master, began to work on the keel of the vessel, which it was determined should be a sloop thirty feet long, and twelve feet wide. This day also the smith finished his forge, and laid in a quantity of fir for fuel: He and the carpenter thenceforward continued to work with indefatigable diligence, except when prevented by the weather. The smith having fortunately found the ring and nut of a bower anchor, which served him for an anvil, supplied chisels, axes, hammers, and nails, as they were required; and the carpenter used them with great dexterity and dispatch, until the 31st of the month, when he fell sick.

As the lives of the whole company were dependent on the carpenter's safety, they watched his recovery with the utmost impatience and anxiety; and to their unspeakable joy, his convalescence was such on 2 August, as to enable him to return to work.

Meantime the stores which had been saved from the wreck were so nearly exhausted, that it was necessary to restrict each man to an allowance of two ounces of bread a-day, while water also fell short. It was resolved to keep the salt pork to victual the new vessel.

In this distressing state they had recourse to several expedients. In digging a well they were disappointed in their hopes of finding a spring; but they succeeded in knocking down some of the gannets that settled on the top of the rock. The flesh, however, was very rank, of a fishy taste, and as black as a sloe. They also made a catamaran or float, on which they proposed to go out fishing with such hooks and lines as had come ashore. Likewise they killed some seals, but all who ate of them were sick.

When driven to great necessity, they killed a hog; they generally had success in fishing, and sometimes sent out two rafts at a time. On one occasion, Mr Collet, and Mr Yets, the midshipman, were nearly driven out to sea, while engaged in this manner, where they would have infallibly perished. They had been out fishing on the 20th of August until about four in the afternoon, when they weighed and endeavoured to come in again; but the wind suddenly freshening from the westward, they found that instead of gaining ahead they drove off very fast. Though the people on shore saw their distress, they knew not how to assist them; however, they sent out another float with kellicks and ropes, which they hoped would enable them to ride till the wind moderated. The surf, however, was so great, that the raft overset three times, and the men were obliged to swim back. In the interval they saw their friends driving out to sea at a great rate, and were just giving them up to inevitable destruction, when the carpenter sent them word that he could make the little boat so tight that she should not take in water faster than one man could bale out. This inspired them with new hopes, and every one was ready to venture to the assistance of their comrades. In quarter of an hour the carpenter dispatched the boat, and she soon overtook the float, when she received the two people. They now found that the water gained very fast on them, notwithstanding their utmost efforts, and when the boat came in, she was so full, that in a few minutes more she must have sunk.

As they were afraid to venture any longer on a raft, the carpenter again set to work on the boat, and put her into complete repair. Their success in fishing was very uncertain; sometimes they caught nothing; nor were their supplies on shore less precarious; the gannets would sometimes settle in amazing numbers like a cloud, and then totally disappear for several days together. This rendered them very desirous of finding some way to preserve the food they caught, from putrefaction, that they might store up the surplus of a successful day to serve when neither gannets nor fish were to be caught. They made several abortive attempts to cure both fish and fowl by smoking, and then tried to make salt, which had like to have been fatal to them all. The smith had made a copper vessel for the experiment, and they immediately set to work, not knowing that their process in making salt would produce verdigris from the copper, and that it was poison. Salt nevertheless was procured, but the substance rendering it poisonous, happened to abound in such a degree as to render it intolerably offensive to the taste, and it was on that account thrown away. Those who ventured to swallow it, were seized with violent colics, cold sweats, and retchings, which sufficiently convinced them of the danger they had escaped.

On Wednesday 3 September, these unfortunate people had been inhabitants of this desolate rock nearly seven weeks; during which time they had frequently seen a great smoke on the main land, which made them extremely anxious to send the boat thither to see what assistance could be obtained.

Therefore Bothwell, Rosenbury, and Taylor, this day set out on a voyage of discovery; and at night the people ashore made a great fire on the highest part of the rock as a signal to them.

While waiting the return of the boat, they were all thrown into the utmost consternation by an accident which befell the carpenter. He unluckily cut his leg in such a manner with an adze, that he was in great danger of bleeding to death, as they had no surgeon among them, nor any thing fit for applying to the wound. At length the blood was staunched, though with much difficulty, and the wound healed, without the intervention of any bad symptom.

The weather having been fair for forty hours, the return of the boat was impatiently expected on Saturday 6 September. As nothing was seen of her against noon, the people became very uneasy; but just as they were sitting down to dinner, they were agreeably surprised by two of their number, who came running over the rocks to announce her approach. All starting up, overjoyed at the intelligence, ran to see her come in, entertaining great hopes that the excursion had succeeded. But they soon distinguished that she was rowed by only one man, who plied both oars, and thence concluded that the other two were either lost or detained. Presently another was seen rising from the bottom of the boat, where it was supposed he had lain down for a short interval of rest, and then the boat advanced somewhat quicker, though yet slowly.

Dinner was now entirely forgot, and after they had waited an hour on the beach with the utmost impatience, the boat came in. The two men were Rosenbury and Taylor, who, the moment of landing, threw themselves on their knees, uttering short but earnest ejaculations of thanks to God, for having once more brought them safe to this place, which, barren and desolate as it was, they considered an asylum from a more distressing situation. Having exerted their last effort to bring the boat to the shore, their strength at once forsook them, and they were unable to rise from the ground without assistance.

As soon as they were conducted over to the tent, every one was busy to procure them refreshment, for they found the boat quite empty both of provisions and water. Some fish was hastily dressed, and their comrades observing them quite

exhausted by labour and watching, left them without asking
any questions, when they had ate their meal, and they
immediately fell asleep. The behaviour of this unfortunate
company to their poor messmates, was an uncommon
instance of kindness and self-denial. The impatience of their
curiosity must have increased in proportion as they were
interested in the account by which it was to be gratified. Yet
even this curiosity, where the very preservation of life was
concerned, they had the consideration and fortitude to
repress, rather than delay the refreshment of the others to
satisfy it.

When the two adventurers awoke, their account was of the
following purport:

About three o'clock on the day of their departure, they got
round a point about six leagues east of the rock, which, as they
approached, had the appearance of a double point. This
encouraged them to hope, that between the two points they
should find a harbour; but here they were disappointed, as a
high surf ran all along the coast. However, about five o'clock,
having seen only one of the natives, they ventured to pull in for
the shore; but the moment they got into the surf, the boat
overset, by which accident Bothwell was unhappily drowned.
They themselves who reached the shore in a feeble and
exhausted condition, were left destitute of every supply except
a small keg of brandy. As soon as their strength was a little
renewed, they crawled along the shore in search of the boat,
having no other chance of shelter from the wild beasts, which
might be expected to come abroad in the night. After some
search they found her, but were too weak to get her up; and
darkness coming on, they were obliged to lie down on the
sand, without any other covering than the branches of a tree,
in which condition they passed the night. As morning dawned
they again went in quest of the boat, which the surf had driven
from the place where they left her. Walking along the coast,
they saw a man, who, on their advancing towards him, ran
away into very thick woods near the beach. Proceeding
onwards, they, in a short time, discovered the body of their
comrade, Bothwell, which had been dragged up the sand a
considerable distance from the water, and was torn to pieces

by some wild beast. This terrified them exceedingly, and having found the boat, the dread of passing another night on shore was so great, that they resolved immediately to return.

The two adventurers were opposed in this attempt by a fresh gale at west, and before they could put back, the boat overset a second time, and drove with them along the shore. After much struggling and swimming, they once more got safe on the land, though fainting with hunger and fatigue, as they had been fasting ever since three o'clock of the preceding day. However, they happened to meet with a fruit resembling an apple, which they eagerly gathered and ate, without knowing either its name or its quality. Fortunately it did them no harm, and being somewhat refreshed by this repast, they made shift to haul the boat on shore. Turning it upside down, they crept under it to sleep, well sheltered from the sun, and secure against wild beasts.

Those who know the irresistible power of sleep, after long watching and excessive labour, will not conclude that their first slumber was short, because their situation was incommodious, or exposed to danger. They wakened, however, before the next morning, and peeping out from under the edge of the boat, could discern the feet of several creatures, which, by the claws, they supposed to be tigers, pass by them to and again. This was a sufficient inducement to remain in their resting place until morning, when once more looking out they saw the feet of a man. On this discovery, they crept from below the boat, to the great amazement of a poor savage, and two other men and a boy, who were at some distance. When they had all collected, and were a little recovered from their surprise, they made signs to the sailors to go away, which they endeavoured to do, though able to move but very slowly. Before having got far from the boat, a considerable number of the natives ran down upon them, with their lances. Rosenbury, as he went along, had picked up the mast of the boat, and a pistol, which had been washed ashore. Thus armed when the Indians came down upon him, and besides being unable to run, he imprudently turned about, and exerting all his strength, advanced towards them in a threatening manner, supposing they would have been panic struck, and retreated into the woods. It happened, however, that he was mistaken, for instead of running away, they surrounded him, and began to whet their lances. Taylor thought it was now time to try what could be done by supplication, and, throwing himself on his knees, cried, in a piteous tone, for mercy, while Rosenbury took refuge in the water. The savages immediately came up to Taylor, and began to strip him. He suffered them quietly to take his shoes and his shirt, but when they attacked his trousers, he made some resistance, and by his gestures entreated that they would not leave him quite naked, on which they thought fit to desist. They then made signs for Rosenbury to come to them, who was all this time swimming about in the sea; but he refused, signifying that they would kill him. They then pointed to Taylor, intimating that he had not been killed; on which Rosenbury advanced, and having first thrown them his pistol, and all his clothes but his shirt, ventured to put himself in their hands. When he came up they offered him no violence, only held the boat's mast and the pistols to him by way of deriding his attempt to frighten them. They seemed to be very much pleased with the clothes, which they divided among themselves as far as they would go. Then beginning to rifle the boat, they took away all the rope they could find, and the hook by which the rudder hung to the stern post, and next began to knock the stern to pieces, for the iron which they saw about it. Except absolute destruction of the unfortunate mariners, this was the greatest mishap they could sustain; and rough as they were, they burst into tears, entreating the savages, with such agony of distress, to desist from injuring their boat, that they suffered it to remain as they found it. Encouraged by such an appearance of placability and kindness, and urged by hunger, they solicited by signs something to eat. This request was also granted, and the natives having given them some roots, again made signs for their departure; on which they once more got into the boat, after launching it; but the wind blowing strong from the west, they could not put off. The natives perceiving their willingness, and also they inability to comply with their desire, covered them with the boat to sleep under, and left them. The following morning the weather proving fine, and the wind easterly, they launched the boat a third time, and returned back to the rock.

The carpenter and smith now continued working on the vessel, till the fourth Sunday, the 29th of September, and the people were busy in securing what was from time to time thrown up by the wreck, particularly cordage and canvas for rigging. They likewise recovered some casks of fresh water, which they were solicitous to keep for sea store, as their escape depended no less on fresh water than on the vessel itself, which was to carry them.

This day, the officers, after prayers, a duty regularly and publicly performed every Sunday, discovered that the chest of treasure had been broke open, and the greater part of it taken away and concealed. It may probably appear strange, that those whom danger had made religious should at the same time be guilty of theft; but it should here be remembered, that as soon as a ship is lost, the sailors lose their pay, and the captain his command; and whatever is cast ashore from the wreck, is considered by the sailors in the light of common property. The men, therefore, who ventured secretly to take what they deemed their share of this treasure, were not conscious of acting dishonestly, but only designed to secure what they dreaded the officers would monopolize, and thus prevent disputes, which, in their circumstances, might produce fatal effects. The officers, however, on discovering what had been done, and finding that none would own knowing any thing about it, proposed to write the form of an oath, and administer it separately to every individual, themselves taking it first. But to this the majority immediately objected, for though they might not suppose themselves guilty of a crime by taking the treasure, they were aware that it would not only be immoral but impious, to swear they had not taken it. As the minority were not in a condition to enforce their proposal, the matter was suffered to rest without further inquiry or remonstrance.

A fowling-piece was found on 6 October, which was a joyful acquisition, and although the barrel was much beat, it was soon made serviceable by the carpenter, and used with great success in shooting the birds. There was no other method before of taking them, but by knocking them down with a stick.

On Friday 11 October, the gannets which had of late forsaken the rock, were observed again hovering about it in great numbers. The shipwrecked people were therefore in hopes that they would settle to lay their eggs, and in this they were not disappointed. They were constantly supplied with great plenty of eggs, until the beginning of January, when the laying season terminated.

Mr Cottes, Mr Webb, the third mate, and two others, once more ventured out on a raft on the 20th of October, but the wind springing up very fresh, the raft broke loose, and drove them to the other side of the rocks. The sea running high, and the wind still increasing, it was impossible for the boat to put out; therefore they were obliged to remain all night among the seals on the rocks, without any shelter or refreshment. But in this situation, however dreadful, they received great comfort, for reflecting how much more dangerous it would have been, had they, instead of being carried to the rocks, been driven out to sea. The wind did not abate before next day at noon, when the boat ventured off: but as the waves still ran high, it could bring in no more than two at a time, and the float was left behind them.

Some rainy weather now prevailed, which was very acceptable, as they contrived to save some of the water for sea store; but they were still in want of bread, and had lived many days on short allowance. As a last resource, they thought of building an oven, for though they had no bread they had some barrels of flour. In this attempt they succeeded beyond expectation, and were enabled to convert their flour into tolerable biscuit.

At length the biscuit also was near exhausted, and their allowance of it restricted to a few ounces per day, without brandy, of which only a small quantity remained, and this was preserved inviolable for the use of the carpenter. Water likewise ran short, and a pint a day was all their allowance. However, their health still remained in a great measure entire; and on 16 February 1756, they launched their vessel, which they called the *Happy Deliverance*. Next day, their little pittance of stores was got on board, and on the 18th they set sail from the rock, which, at parting, they named *Bird Island*, and where they had lived just seven months.

All their provisions consisted of six casks of water, two live hogs, a firkin of butter, about four pounds of biscuit for each man, and ten days subsistence of salt provisions, in bad condition, at the rate of two ounces a day per man.

At one in the afternoon of the eighteenth, the adventurers weighed anchor, and with a light breeze from the west, set sail for the river St Lucia, on the coast of Natal. Fortune, however, did not cease to persecute them: for five days they met nothing but adversity; and during twenty-five in succession, their provisions were almost exhausted, and currents running at the rate of a mile and a half an hour carried them so far out of their course, that a favourable wind was of little avail. Their state became more and more deplorable, and they at length despaired of reaching the river St Lucia; as the currents ran strong to the west, and easterly winds almost always prevailed, they resolved to change their course, and attempt to make the Cape of Good Hope. Thus on 2 March they bore away to the west.

Next day the weather proved hazy, and they apprehended that heavy westerly gales would ensue. Their conjectures were verified, for the wind increased to prodigious violence, until the fourth of the month, when they endeavoured to lie to, but shipped such heavy seas that they dreaded lest every surge would dash their slight vessel to pieces; thus they were still obliged to be cautious, and bear away under a topsail. The squalls were at times so violent that the sea appeared like cliffs above the stern; and in this alarming manner were they hurried along by furious storms until the morning of the fifth, when fine weather ensued.

A calm prevailed on the seventh, and they cast anchor about three quarters of a mile from a shore, where they soon observed several of the natives, who came down from the mountains. Encouraged by this sight, they attempted to land; and Thomas Arnold, the black servant, accompanied by two seamen, embarked in the boat, carrying a string of amber beads as a present to the Indians. Arnold leapt out of the boat when near the beach, and swam ashore, while the boat returned to the vessel, which was standing on at some distance in search of a place where the people might safely debark. Attended by about forty of the natives, Arnold followed the vessel to a suitable place, and the boat was sent to take him off. He reported that on his arrival, the savages at first appeared very reserved, but, at length, having all sat down, they made him sit down among them. He then presented the string of beads to the oldest, who received it with marks of consideration. On making signs that he wanted food, they supplied him with Indian corn, fruit, and water, in a calabash. He added that they had sent into the country for sheep, oxen, and other necessaries, whence he was desirous of returning to them; but the wind continuing westerly, the boat only was sent ashore, which soon returned with food sufficient to serve during four days.

The vessel coasted along until 10 March, when the wind changed to the east, and the people then cast anchor in twelve fathoms, half a mile from the shore. Several Indians came down to the beach in the evening, and by signs invited them to land, which they considered impracticable. Next morning the natives renewed their invitation, by driving before them a great many goats and bullocks. This was a pleasing spectacle to men almost famished with hunger; however, they still judged it impossible to land. In a condition so tantalising they continued until the 14th, when two men requested to be sent ashore at all risks, saying it was better to go and live among the savages than to perish of hunger on board, where for two days they had not ate a morsel. They were therefore sent off in the boat, and with great difficulty reached the shore. The wind fell the same evening, and seemed tending to the west, which occasioned much uneasiness to those on board, on account of their two comrades ashore, for they dreaded that it might blow too hard for them to remain at anchor until morning. Thus frequent signals were made through the night by shewing lights, in hopes of bringing them down to the beach, that they might get off before the surf rose too high. No intelligence was obtained of them until six in the morning, but it was then too late to get them on board from the violence of the wind and height of the surf. Trusting to find some more favourable place whence to take them in, signals were made that they should proceed along the shore, while the bark followed the same direction. They had not advanced two leagues, when a very convenient spot was found, opposite to which the vessel, working close to the shore, anchored in five fathoms water. The boat was then sent out, with four men, two of whom were employed in recovering those ashore, and the other two in sounding the mouth of a river, where they were in great hopes of finding water enough for the vessel to pass over the bar. About three hours afterwards, the two men were seen with the four belonging to the boat, but on account of the height of the surf they durst not embark.

All those on board spent the night in the greatest uneasiness; at break of day, they weighed anchor, and stood still nearer the shore; but observing that their companions were still afraid to venture, they made them understand that if they did not immediately return, or shew that it was possible to enter the river, they should be obliged to abandon them, as provisions began to fail, and there was no appearance of any here. These menaces had the desired effect, and two of the men braved the extreme violence of the surf in the boat. Having gained the bark, they said that they had been well received by the natives, who gave them beef and fish to eat, and supplied them with milk; and then conducted them over the mountains, from the place where they landed, to that where they found their companions.

An easterly wind rendered it dangerous to remain in this spot, but was favourable for their entering the river, where sufficient water was said to be above the bar; accordingly, they weighed anchor at eleven in the forenoon, and advanced, the boat always being before, sounding. But when close to the bar, those ashore made signals to desist; which they did, and anchored. The boat returning, informed them that there were only eight feet of water on the bar, and that it was necessary to wait the flowing of the tide in order to pass it. At two in the afternoon, they once more hoisted sail, easily entered the river, and cast anchor in two fathoms and a half.

Their first consideration was how to traffic with the natives for provisions and other necessaries, having never heard of any commerce on this coast. The consultation did not continue long, for they had but little to exchange; their whole stock, consisting of brass buttons, nails, and iron bolts, copper hoops, of which they made rings, such as are called bangles by the Indians, and wore as bracelets on the legs and arms. These they carried on shore, and shewing them to the natives, made signs by imitating the lowing of cattle, and bleating of sheep, that they wished these animals in exchange for them. The Indians quickly comprehended their meaning, and speedily brought two small oxen, which were purchased for a pound of copper and three or four brass buttons. Each of the oxen weighed about five or six hundred pounds, and the flesh proved excellent. The Indians seemed well content with their bargain, and promised to bring more cattle; they likewise sold a great quantity of milk at a very low rate, demanding but a single button for two or three gallons. They also sold, at the same rate, a quantity of small grain resembling Guinea corn, which the strangers bruising between two stones, made into a kind of bread, which they baked on hot cinders. This they were in hopes to preserve, until they could procure what was of better quality, but here they were disappointed, for in three days it became mouldy. Nevertheless, the grain was found salutary food when boiled along with meat.

In this place they remained about fifteen days, and frequently penetrated the country, ten or twelve miles, to the dwellings of the natives, who lived in huts covered with rushes, which formed a kind of thatch. They were extremely clean within, and the natives frequently invited their visitors to spend the night there, during their residence on the coast. They always testified great friendship towards the English, often ate along with them, and seemed to enjoy the European method of preparing food. But they particularly prized the entrails of animals, which they commonly ate raw, after giving them a shake. They also took much pleasure in going on board the vessel, and repeatedly came up the river in the boat along with the English, uniformly displaying a very sociable disposition. They shewed no jealousy, and left their sisters and daughters whole days with the strangers, while rambling about the woods.

Hunting is the principal occupation of these savages; their only weapons are lances, and two short clubs, with a large knob at the end, which are used to kill an animal when it is wounded by the lance. The river is full of manatees, or sea-cows, which commonly come to the banks and pasture in the night; they are quite harmless, and the natives frequently kill them for food while asleep.

They also had a few elephant's tusks, which they would have given for a mere trifle, but the English had no room for them in the vessel. These savages wore few clothes in the day-time, but at night covered themselves with a bullock's hide, which was well dried, and which they had the art of rendering very pliant. Their chief ornaments were a piece of the tail of an ox, which hung from the rump, down to their heels, and was adorned with small sea-shells. They also wore pieces of skin round the knees, ankles, and arms. Their hair was anointed with abundance of fat or grease, mixed with a kind of red earth, and the whole body was likewise anointed. Their activity and address were so great in throwing their lances, that at the distance of thirty or forty yards, they could strike an ear of corn set up as a mark. They practised another exercise, particularly at meeting each other, or on separation, which consisted in dancing or leaping in a circle, and uttering the most hideous cries, sometimes like hounding of dogs, and sometimes like the grunting of hogs, all the while actively wielding their lances.

The English were extremely surprised to find among these savages, who were a quite black with woolly hair, a youth, apparently twelve or fourteen years of age, perfectly white, with European features, fine light hair, and altogether different from the natives of this country. They remarked that he was treated as a servant, that the savages sent him their errands, and sometimes did not allow him to eat with them; but that he waited until the end of their repast, before making his own. They seemed, at the same time, to live in great friendship with each other, and when they had any thing to

eat, though in ever so small a quantity, the owner shared it
equally with all present, and appeared to enjoy much
satisfaction in doing so.

After the English had thus, by the intervention of
Providence, collected a very considerable quantity of
provisions, they weighed anchor at five in the morning of the
29th, and stood over the bar. But there a dangerous surf was
running, which almost broke into the vessel, and becalming
their sail, put them in great hazard of being shipwrecked on
the rocks. At length they had the good fortune to get over the
bar, and sailed for the River St Lucia, where they arrived on
the 6th of April, without any remarkable occurrence.

Having landed, they were soon convinced that those with
whom they were to traffic, were very different from the savages
they had left. On signifying that they wished to trade with
them, the Indians intimated that they wanted no commodity
but a kind of small beads; nevertheless, when shown copper
buttons, they speedily brought several bullocks, fowls,
potatoes, gourds, and some other provisions. No bullocks
could be purchased, because the natives demanded copper
rings large enough for collars, in exchange; but they sold fowls
and gourds at a low price, giving five or six of the former, of a
large size, for a bit of linen, not worth above fourpence in
England.

Here the English remained three weeks, occupying
themselves in traversing the country, and in seeing the
savages' mode of life, as also in endeavouring to obtain the
articles they required. These Indians put the highest value on
copper; and, on being shewn the handle of an old box, offered
two bullocks for it; the bargain was speedily concluded, and
they drove them to the bark. The natives appeared very proud
and haughty, and quite different in the recommendatory
manners that characterized those whom the English had
lately left. The latter discovered that the principal chief, whom
they paid for being accommodated all night in one of his huts,
had stolen some pieces of iron, which they had brought in a
basket, to discharge their expenses while ashore. Though they
remained two or three days in the interior, the natives could
never be prevailed on to eat along with their visitors. They

differed also from the former Indians in the method of preparing their food, which was here done with greater neatness; they were likewise more cleanly in their persons, and bathed every morning, apparently as an act of devotion, nothing of which was observed among the others. They wore no kind of ornament; their chief pride seemed to be to keep their hair in great order. They watched strictly over their women. Their arms, however, resembled those of the others, as did their diversions. Men were seen among them, who came from Delagoa, trading in ambergris and elephant's tusks.

A favourable breeze springing up from the west, attended with good weather, the English weighed anchor, at seven in the morning of the 18th of May, and set sail. About a quarter of an hour before high water, when almost on a bar crossing the river, some of them were so imprudent as to lower the sail, and cast anchor on a sandbank. Nine men then got into the boat and rowed towards the shore, declaring they would rather run all risks among the savages, than be drowned to a certainty in passing the bar. Those on board hesitated whether to attempt the passage, or return; but the wind and tide driving the vessel out of the river, gave every reason to believe, that if the tide fell, she would strike the bar and be dashed to pieces. At length they weighed anchor, trusting to save the vessel and preserve their lives, and were soon carried among the breakers. Here they were in the most alarming situation, there were only eight feet of water, while the vessel drew five. After remaining half an hour in the jaws of death, the surface of the sea suddenly became smooth as glass, and they left the River St Lucia in safety. Those ashore, most of whom had nothing but a shirt and a pair of trousers, followed along the coast on foot.

On the 20th of the month the English made Delagoa River, where they cast anchor in nine fathoms. There they found the *Rose*, a snow, commanded by Captain Chandler, in which some of them requested a passage to Bombay. Having remained three weeks in this place, three of their comrades, who had gone ashore at St Lucia, rejoined them in a small canoe, and said that their six companions were on the other side of Delagoa Bay, from whence they waited an opportunity of coming over.

The officers, judging themselves now in the most convenient

situation for securing the treasure, packets, and other effects of
the *Doddington*, sent four or five men ashore, and two on board
the snow. Mr Jones then came in Captain Chandler's pinnace,
well manned and armed, to the vessel, and carried all the
money, plate, and letters, he could find in her, to the snow,
that they might be given up on her arrival at Madras. The
people remaining in the vessel, apprehending a second visit,
which might have been extremely disagreeable, took an
opportunity of escaping during the night.

The *Rose* sailed for Madagascar on the 25th of May, for the
purpose of completing her cargo, as, in consequence of a
misunderstanding between Captain Chandler and the natives,
they had driven away above an hundred head of cattle after
having sold them to him. On the same day, a vessel came in
sight, which, on approaching, proved to be the bark. Two of
the people, one of whom was the carpenter, coming on board
the snow, persuaded Captain Chandler to purchase their little
vessel for five hundred rupees, and he gave his note for that
sum. They told him that they had recovered the other six men
who had gone ashore at St Lucia, but three of that party were
already dead, and two extremely ill, from the fatigues they
had suffered in travelling by land. These also died a few days
afterwards. Captain Chandler then continued his course to
Madagascar, in company with the bark, and, after a voyage of
twenty-two days, discovered the island, where he anchored,
off Morondova, on the 14th of June. The *Caernarvon*,
commanded by Norton Hutchinson, bound from Europe for
China, likewise arrived there on the 16th.

The packets and treasure being destined for Madras, they
were put on board this vessel, which quitted Morondova on
the 1st of July, and, having arrived a month afterwards at that
government, the whole were delivered according to their
original destination.

8

Damsel in Distress

The miseries of war are in themselves great and terrible, but the consequences which arise indirectly from it, though seldom known and little adverted to, are no less deplorable. The destruction of the sword sometimes bears only an inconsiderable proportion to the havoc of disease, and, in the pestilential climates of the western colonies, entire regiments, reared in succession, have as often fallen victims to their baneful influence.

To prosecute the war with alacrity, it had been judged expedient to transport a strong body of troops on foreign service, but their departure was delayed by repeated adversities, and at length the catastrophe which is about to be related ensued.

On 15 November 1795, the fleet, under convoy of Admiral Christian's squadron, sailed from St Helen's. A more beautiful sight than it exhibited cannot be conceived; and those who had nothing to lament in leaving their native country, enjoyed the spectacle as the most magnificent produced by the art of man, and as that which the natives of this island contemplate with mingled pride and pleasure.

Next day, the wind continuing favourable, carried the fleet down the Channel; and as the *Catharine* transport came within sight of the isle of Purbeck, Lieutenant Jenner, an officer on board, pointed out to another person the rocks where the *Halsewell* and so many unfortunate individuals had perished. He and Cornet Burns had been unable to reach Southampton until the *Catharine* had sailed, therefore they hired a hoy to overtake her, and on embarking at St Helen's the former expressed his satisfaction, in a letter to his mother, that he had been so fortunate as to do so.

On Tuesday the 17th, the fleet was off Portland, standing to the westward; but the wind shifting and blowing a strong gale at south-south-west, the admiral, dubious whether they could clear the Channel, made a signal for putting into Torbay, which some of the transports were then in sight of. However, they could not make the bay; the gale increased, and a thick fog came on; therefore the admiral thought it expedient to alter his design, and about five in the afternoon made a signal for standing out to sea. Of the circumstances relative to the *Catharine*, a more detailed account has been preserved than respecting the other vessels of his fleet; and they are preserved by a female, with whose name we are unacquainted, in these words:

The evening of the 17th was boisterous and threatening; the master said he was apprehensive that we should have bad weather; and when I was desired to go on deck and look at the appearance of the sky, I observed that it was troubled and red, with great heavy clouds flying in all directions, and with a sort of dull mist surrounding the moon. On repeating this to the other passengers, two of whom had been at sea before, they said we should certainly have a stormy night, and indeed it proved so very tempestuous that no rest was to be obtained. Nobody, however, seemed to think there was any danger, though the fog was so thick that the master could see nothing by which to direct his course; but he thought that he had sufficient sea-room.

The fatigue I had suffered from the tossing of the ship, and the violence with which she continued to roll, had kept me in bed. It was about ten o'clock in the morning of the 18th, when the mate looked down into the cabin and cried, 'Save yourselves if you can!'

The consternation and terror of that moment cannot be described; I had on a loose dressing gown, and wrapping it round me I went up, not quite on deck, but to the top of the stairs, from whence I saw the sea break mountains high against the shore. The passengers and soldiers seemed thunderstruck by the sense of immediate and inevitable danger, and the seamen, too conscious of the hopelessness of any exertion, stood in speechless agony, certain of meeting in a few minutes that destruction which now menaced them.

While I thus surveyed the scene around me in a kind of dread which no words can figure, Mr Burns, an officer of the dragoons, who had come up in his shirt, called to Mr Jenner and Mr Stains for his cloak; nobody, however, could attend to any thing in such a moment but self-preservation.

Mr Jenner, Mr Stains, and Mr Dodd the surgeon, now passed me, their countenances sufficiently expressing their sense of the situation in which we all were. Mr Burns spoke cheerfully to me; he bade me take good courage, and Mr Jenner observed, there was a good shore near, and all would do well.

These gentlemen then went to the side of the ship, with the intention, as I believe, of seeing whether it was possible to get on shore. The master of the vessel alone remained near the companion; when suddenly a tremendous wave broke over the ship, and struck me with such violence, that I was stunned for a moment, and, before being able to recover myself, the ship herself struck with a force so great as to throw me from the stairs into the cabin, the master also being thrown down near me. At the same instant, the cabin, with a dreadful crash, broke in upon us, and planks and beams threatened to bury us in ruins. The master, however, soon recovered himself; he left me to go again upon deck, and I saw him no more.

A sense of my condition lent me strength to disengage myself from the boards, and fragments by which I was surrounded, and I once more got up the stairs, I hardly know how. But what a scene did I behold! The masts were all lying across the shattered remains of the deck, and no living creature appeared on it; all were gone, though I knew not then they were gone for ever. I looked forward to the shore, but there I could see nothing except the dreadful surf that broke against it, while, behind the ship, immense black waves rose like tremendous ruins. I knew that they must overwhelm her, and thought that there could be no escape for me.

Believing, then, that death was immediate and unavoidable, my idea was to regain my bed in the cabin, and there, resigning myself to the will of God, await the approaching moment. However, I could not reach it, and for a while was insensible; then the violent striking and breaking up of the

wreck again roused me to recollection. I found myself near the
cabin windows, and the water was rising round me. It rapidly
increased, and the horrors of drowning were present to my
view: yet do I remember seeing the furniture of the cabin
floating about. I sat almost enclosed by pieces of the wreck,
and the water now reached my breast.

The bruises I had received made every exertion extremely
difficult, and my loose gown was so entangled among the
beams and fragments of the ship, that I could not disengage it.
Still the desire of life, the hope of being welcomed on shore,
whither I thought my friends had escaped, and the
remembrance of my child, all united in inspiring me with
courage to attempt saving myself. I again tried to loosen my
gown, but found it impossible, and the wreck continued to
strike so violently, and the ruins to close so much more around
me, that I now expected to be crushed to death.

As the ship drifted higher on the stones, the water rather
lessened as the waves went back, but on their return continued
to cover me, and I once or twice lost my breath, and, for a
moment, my recollection. When I had power to think, the
principle of self-preservation still urged me to exertion.

The cabin now broke more and more, and, through a large
breach, I saw the shore very near me. Amidst the tumult of the
raging waves I had a glimpse of the people, who were
gathering up what the sea drove towards them; but I thought
they could not see me, and from them I despaired of assistance.
Therefore I determined to make an effort to preserve my life. I
disengaged my arms from the dressing-gown, and, finding
myself able to move, I quitted the wreck, and felt myself on the
ground. I attempted to run, but was too feeble to save myself
from a raging wave, which overtook and overwhelmed me.
Then I believed myself gone; yet, half-suffocated as I was, I
struggled very much, and I remember that I thought I was very
long of dying. The wave left me; I breathed again, and made
another attempt to get higher upon the bank, but, quite
exhausted, I fell down, and my senses forsook me.

By this time I was observed by some of the people on the
bank, and two men came to my assistance. They lifted me up:
I once more recovered some faint recollection; and, as they
bore me along, I was sensible that one of them said the sea
would overtake us; that he must let me go and take care of his
own life. I only remember clinging to the other and imploring

him not to abandon me to the merciless waves. But I have a
very confused idea of what passed, till I saw the boat, into
which I was to be put to cross the Fleet water: I had then just
strength to say, 'For God's sake do not take me to sea again.'

I believe the apprehension of it, added to my other sufferings
tended to deprive me of all further sensibility, for I have not the
least recollection of any thing afterwards until roused by the
remedies applied to restore me in a farmhouse whither I was
carried. There I heard a number of women around me, who
asked a great many questions, which I was unable to answer. I
remember hearing one say I was a Frenchwoman; another say
that I was a negro; and indeed I was so bruised, and in such a
disfigured condition, that the conjectures of those people are
not surprising.

When recovering some degree of confused recollection, and
able to speak, I begged they would allow me to go to bed. This,
however, I did not ask with any expectation of life, for I was
now in such a state of suffering, that my only wish was to be
allowed to lie down and die in peace.

Nothing could exceed the humanity of Mr Abbot, the
inhabitant of Fleet farmhouse, nor the compassionate
attention of his sister, Miss Abbot, who not only afforded me
immediate assistance, but continued for some days to attend
me with such kindness and humanity, as I shall always
remember with the sincerest gratitude.

The unfortunate sufferer who gives the preceding account,
was attended with great humanity by Mr Bryer, while a
wound in her foot, and the dangerous bruises she had
received, prevented her from quitting the shelter she first
found under the roof of Mr Abbot, at Fleet. As soon as she was
in a condition to be removed to Weymouth, Mr Bryer, a
surgeon there, received her into his own house, where Mrs
Bryer assisted in administering to her recovery such
benevolent offices of consolation as her deplorable situation
admitted. Meantime, the gentlemen of the south battalion of
the Gloucester Militia, who had done everything possible
towards the preservation of those who were the victims of the
tempest, now liberally contributed to alleviate the pecuniary
distresses of the survivors. None seemed to have so forcible a
claim on their pity as this forlorn and helpless stranger; and

she alone, of forty souls, except a single ship-boy, survived the wreck of the *Catharine*. There perished twelve seamen, two soldiers' wives, twenty-two dragoons, and four officers, Lieutenant Stains, Mr Dodd of the hospital-staff, Lieutenant Jenner, the representative of an ancient and respectable family in Gloucester, aged thirty-one, Cornet Burns, the son of an American loyalist of considerable property, who was deprived of every thing for his adherence to the British Government. Having no dependence but on the promises of government to indemnify those who had suffered on that account, he, after years of distress and difficulty obtained a cornetcy in the 26th regiment of dragoons, then going to the West Indies, and was thus lost in his twenty-fourth year. This officer had intended embarking in another transport, and had actually sent his horse on board, when finding the *Catharine* more commodious, he gave her the preference, while the other put back to Spithead in safety. The mangled remains of Lieutenant Jenner were two days afterwards found on the beach, and interred with military honours.

9

The Cannibals

The following narrative affords a serious warning to men in public service not to allow themselves to be led astray from their duty, or be seduced from their native government, to which they owe allegiance. Temptation, indeed, is often thrown in their way, and there can be no characteristic more truly descriptive of the inhabitants of the British dominions, than that their services are coveted by other kingdoms.

The reputed adventures of six deserters from the island of St Helena, produced a court of inquiry concerning the truth of them, on 12 December 1801, when John Brown, one of the survivors, gave a recital on oath of the events that had befallen them.

In June 1799, Brown belonged to the first company of artillery in the service of the garrison of St Helena. On the 10th of that month, M'Kinnon, the gunner, and an orderly of the second company, about half an hour before parade-time, asked him if he was willing to go on board an American ship called the *Columbia*, Captain Henry Lelar, then the only ship in the roads. After some conversation Brown agreed to do so, and met him towards seven o'clock at the playhouse. There he found four persons about to engage in the same way, one being named M'Quin, a man of Major Seale's company, another called Brighouse, a third Parr, and a fourth Matthew Conway.

Parr was a good seaman, and said he would either take them to the island Ascension, or lie off the harbour of St Helena till the *Columbia* could weigh anchor and get out.

About eight o'clock they went down to the west rocks, where the American boat was waiting for them, manned with three American seamen, who carried them alongside the *Columbia*. They went on board, and, after being there half an hour, changed their clothes. Parr went down to the cabin.

About eleven at night, Brighouse and Conway proposed to cut a whale-boat from out of the harbour, to prevent the *Columbia* being suspected. Accordingly they cut out a boat with a coil of rope in it, five oars, and a large stone, by which it was moored.

Observing lanterns passing on the line towards the sea-gate, and hearing a great noise, they thought they were missed and searched for. They immediately embarked in the whale-boat, with twenty-five pounds of bread in a bag, and a keg of water, containing about thirteen gallons, a compass and a quadrant given to them by the commanding officer of the *Columbia*; but, in the hurry of departure, the quadrant was either left behind or fell overboard.

They then left the ship, pulling with two oars only to get ahead of her; the boat half full of water, and nothing to bale it out. Thus they rowed out to sea, and lay a great distance off, being in hourly expectation of the American ship.

No ship appearing, however, they bore away, about twelve o'clock of the second day, by Parr's advice, steering north by west, and then north-north-west, for the island of Ascension. Their handkerchiefs were used as substitutes for sails, and they met with a gale of wind which lasted two days. The weather then became very fine, and they calculated that they had run towards ten miles an hour. M'Kinnon kept a reckoning with pen, ink, and paper, supplied to him by the *Columbia*, as also charts and maps.

This course was continued until about the 18th, on the morning of which day many birds were seen, but no land. Parr, at twelve o'clock, said that he was sure they must be past the island of Ascension, accounting it to be eight hundred miles from St Helena. Each then gave up his shirt to make a small spritsail of the whole, and they laced their jackets and trousers together at the waistband to keep them warm. Next they altered their course to west by north, thinking to make

Rio de Janeiro on the American coast. Provisions running very short, they restrained themselves to an ounce of bread in twenty-four hours, and two mouthfuls of water.

They continued on the same allowance until the 26th, when all their provisions were consumed. On the 27th M'Quin took a piece of bamboo in his mouth to chew, and all the rest followed his example. It being Brown's turn that night to steer the boat, he cut a piece from one of his shoes, recollecting to have read of people in a similar situation eating their shoes. But he was obliged to spit it out, as it was soaked with salt water; therefore he took the inside sole, part of which he ate, and distributed some to the others. However, it gave them no relief.

On the first of July, Parr caught a dolphin with a gaff that had been left in the boat, on which they all fell on their knees and thanked God for his goodness to them. They tore up the fish and hung it out to dry. On this they subsisted until the fourth, when, finding the whole expended, bones and all, Parr, Brown, Brighouse and Conway proposed to scuttle the boat and let her go down, that they might be put out of their misery. The other two objected, observing that God, who had made man, always found him something to eat.

M'Kinnon, about eleven on the fifth, expressed the opinion that it would be better to cast lots for one of them to die, in order to save the rest, to which they consented. The lots were made; but Parr, having been sick two days with the spotted fever, was excluded. It was his province to write the numbers out and put them into a hat, from which the others, blindfolded, drew them, and put them in their pockets.

Parr then asked whose lot it was to die: none knew what number was in his pocket, but each prayed to God that it might fall on him. It was agreed that he who had number 5 should die; and the lots being unfolded, M'Kinnon's was number 5.

They had previously agreed, that he on whom the lot fell should bleed himself to death, for which purpose they had provided themselves with nails from the boat, which they sharpened. M'Kinnon, with one of them, cut himself in three places, in the foot, hand, and wrist; and, praying God to forgive him, died in about a quarter of an hour.

Before he was quite cold, Brighouse cut a piece of flesh off his thigh, with one of the same nails, and hung it up, leaving his body in the boat. About three hours after they all ate it, but only a very small bit; and the piece lasted until the seventh of the month. Every two hours they dipped the body in the sea in order to preserve it.

Parr having found a piece of slate in the bottom of the boat, sharpened it on the large stone, and cut out another piece of M'Kinnon's thigh with it, which lasted them until the eighth. It was then Brown's watch, and he, observing the water change colour about break of day, called the rest, thinking they were near the shore; but, as it was not quite daylight, they saw no land.

As soon as day appeared, however, they discovered land right a-head, and steered for it, and were close in shore about eight in the morning. There being a very heavy surf, they endeavoured to turn the boat's head to it, which, from weakness, they were unable to accomplish, and soon afterwards the boat upset. Brown, Parr and Conway, got to shore, but M'Quin and Brighouse were drowned.

On the beach a small hut was discovered by the survivors, in which were an Indian and his mother, who informed them that there was a village called Belmont, about three miles distant. The Indian went thither, and gave information that the French had landed; and, in two hours, the governors of the village, a clergyman, along with several armed men, took Conway and Parr prisoners. They tied their hands and feet, and, slinging them on a bamboo stick, carried them in this manner to the village. Brown was extremely weak; he remained in the hut some time, and was afterwards taken.

On the prisoners informing the people that they were English, they were immediately released, and three hammocks provided for them, in which they were carried to the governor's, who allowed them to lie in his own bed, and gave them milk and rice to eat; but they were seized with a locked jaw, from not having eaten any thing for a considerable time, and continued so until the 23rd. In the interval the governor of this place wrote to the governor of St Salvador, who sent a small schooner to Porto Seguro, for the purpose of conveying them to St Salvador.

They were then conducted on horseback through Santa Cruz to Porto Seguro, where they remained about ten days, and after that embarked. On their arrival at St Salvador, Parr, when interrogated by the governor, said he was captain of a ship, the *Sally* of Liverpool, which had·foundered at sea, and that he and his comrades had saved themselves in the boat; that the ship belonged to his father, and was last from Cape Corfe Castle, on the coast of Africa, whence she was to touch at Ascension for turtle, and was then bound for Jamaica.

These three men continued about thirteen days at St Salvador, during which time the inhabitants collected a subscription of L. 200 for each of them. They then embarked in a Portuguese ship for Lisbon, Parr going in the capacity of mate, Conway as boatswain's mate, and Brown, who was sickly, as a passenger. In thirteen days they reached Rio de Janeiro: Parr and Conway sailed for Lisbon, and Brown was left in the hospital.

In about three months, Captain Elphinstone of the *Diomede* pressed Brown into his majesty's service, giving him the choice of remaining on that station, or to proceed to the admiral at the Cape of Good Hope. He preferred the latter, and was put, along with seven suspected deserters, in irons, on board the *Ann*, a Botany Bay ship, with the convicts. When he arrived at the Cape, he was put on board the *Lancaster* of sixty-four guns; he never entered; but at length he received his discharge, after which he engaged in the *Duke of Clarence*, as a seaman, resolving to give himself up at the first opportunity, in order to relate his sufferings to the men of the garrison of St Helena, that they might thereby be deterred from attempting so wild a scheme again.

10

Amazing Grace

September 1838. The *Forfarshire*, 366 tons, the latest type of well-appointed paddle-steamer, built in Dundee only two years before for the Hull and Dundee Steam Packet Co., left Hull for its northward passage on the evening of the 6th, carrying 40 passengers, a crew of 20 (to be precise: 10 seamen, 4 firemen, 2 engineers, 2 coal-trimmers, 2 stewards), and a valuable mixed cargo of hardware, cloth, soap and spinning gear, insured for over £4,000. These were early days of steam afloat, and engines by no means as reliable as they later became. The leaky state of the boilers of this ship led one of the firemen to say later that when he first saw them on leaving Hull, 'I would gladly have swum ashore if I had been able.'

The wind, which had been SSE at the start, backed to the north and gained force through the night. By dint of various engine-room improvisations the ship had all but gained St Abb's Head when the boiler leaks became so unmanageable as to put the fires out finally, and leave the ship helpless. The master, John Humble of Newcastle, whose wife was aboard with him, hoisted sail in an effort to control the southerly drift, but in vain; about 4 a.m. on the 7th the *Forfarshire* was washed onto the Big Harcar (or Harker or Hawker) Rock, one of the largest of the twenty or more islets which make up the Farne (or Fern) Islands, 7 miles off the north Northumberland coast.

The main lighthouse protecting the Farnes was then, as it is today, the Longstone – red with a white stripe, built in 1826 on the outer side of the outermost reef of the Farnes, and lit by an oil lamp with circular wick and reflectors. Its keeper was

88

William Darling, aged 52, who lived with his wife and family on the spot. He had nine children, of whom, as it happened, only one, the seventh, Grace Horsley Darling, aged 22, was at home that night; her two younger twin brothers, William Brooks Darling and George, were pursuing their education on the mainland.

On hitting the Harcar Rock the *Forfarshire* broke in half just aft of the paddle-wheel assembly, all those in the after part of the ship being drowned, the forepart staying wedged in a cleft of the rock. In all 13 passengers and 5 crew were saved, some of these having got away in a lifeboat under the command of the mate James Duncan: this boat drifted for two days before being picked up by the *Margaret & Isabella*, a sloop from Montrose. Another lifeboat was washed up later, empty, in Middlesbrough, and cases of the cargo, together with corpses in varying states of decay, were still floating ashore for days thereafter. Identification was difficult since there was no passenger list, the fares being collected en route.

An inquest was held on 11 September in Bamburgh village on four of the dead. The jury brought in verdicts of accidental death but found that the vessel was unseaworthy when she left Hull and censured the captain as 'culpably negligent in not putting back to port'. (It has been suggested that one of the reasons for Mr Humble wishing to push on at all costs was to save himself his wife's hotel bill for the night if they had returned to Hull.) The wreck was assessed for *deodand* at £100, being half the estimated value of the part of the ship still stuck on the rock; and the remains were later bought by a Dundee shipbreaker for £70. (*Deodand* – 'to be given to God' – was a payment levied by the state on incidents where the damage was 'the misfortune rather than the crime of the owner'. Such payments were abolished in 1846.)

It was deposed at the inquest – though not by the Darlings, who were not present – that Grace's attention had first been drawn to the wreck by 'the screams of the wildfowl disturbed from their resting place'. This was before sunrise; it was 7 a.m. before father and daughter had descried through the mist and rain people still living and moving in the wreckage. They launched their 'coble' rowboat at once, with the help of Mrs

Darling, who probably wondered if she would ever see them alive again. As the crow flies the distance from Longstone to the Harcar is about 360 yards, but the seas were so high that Darling's most expert seamanship was required to bring the coble round to the lee of the rock where the wreck lay, and the round trip must have been well over a mile in the end. Grace's seamanship too was tested to the utmost in preventing the coble itself being dashed to pieces on the rock while her father was ashore investigating the wreck and the survivors, then holding the coble inshore to embark the passengers safely. Eight men and a woman were still alive on the wreck – the last in great distress, having seen her two young children swept away by the sea in front of her. The coble held only five, so that, as Darling had calculated, two journeys had to be made; the second of these was made with the help of the *Forfarshire*'s own crew. Grace stayed at home with her mother to look after the survivors.

Three things need to be emphasised:

(1) The rescue was not made at night, as many romantic painters liked to depict it, but at 7 a.m. after sunrise. It would have been madness for Darling, with or without Grace's help, to put out any earlier. Nor did he know for certain before sunrise, despite constant use of his telescope ('the glass incessantly applied' was his own phrase) that there were living people at the wreck. When he knew, he immediately consulted Grace: 'we agreed that if we could get to them, some of them would be able to assist us back, without which we could not return ... we immediately launched our boat.'

(2) Two other romantic inventions were disposed of by William Darling in a letter he wrote later to a Trinity House enquiry: 'The fiction of Grace Darling's having heard cries from the Harker's rock (a thing impossible) and rousing her Father may have arisen from someone having confounded the wreck of the *Forfarshire* with that of the *Autumn* mentioned before; but the other portions of the popular romancing story of William Darling's deferring to his daughter's entreaties, and so forth, are pure invention.' (During the *Autumn* incident Grace had indeed been alone on watch in the lighthouse tower and roused her father, who took off at once with three of her

brothers.) Attendance at wrecks was a routine chore for the Darling family – indeed on one occasion in 1860, the year of Darling's final retirement, he took his son and two of his grandsons with him in the rescue boat.

(3) There is little doubt that had any of Grace's brothers been at home that night they would have been in the coble, and not Grace. In fact one of her brothers, William Brooks Darling, was doing a shift that night with the lifeboat crew at Seahouses down the coast. Here it was too rough to launch the lifeboat at all; instead they launched another coble, heading into the north wind with great difficulty, and reached the scene of the wreck too late to do anything but collect the dead. It was too rough for this boat to return to Seahouses, so that its crew had to join the *Forfarshire* survivors at the Longstone lighthouse. Thus fourteen persons in all, besides the Darling family, spent three days and nights there; they sheltered as well as they could in the derelict workmen's barracks built to accommodate the masons building the lighthouse in 1826.

None of these working considerations were known at the time to the general public, avid then as now for its heroes – and in consonance with the arrival of the new young Queen Victoria on the throne the year before, for heroines as well. 'Unexampled in the feats of female fortitude' sang the *Newcastle Journal* a week after the event; and *The Times* added its bass to the chorus a week later. Portrait painters (today they would be TV cameramen) hurried to Northumberland – at one time, to her father's disgust, she was sitting to six painters at the same time; she received offers to appear in theatres – all she was asked to do was to sit motionless in her coble on stage for three minutes; a Russian gentleman sent her a miniature of his handsome nephew asking her to kiss it and return it; locks purporting to be her hair were freely sold; a Berwick firm of hatters designed a new black beaver bonnet called the 'Darling Hat'; the Duke of Northumberland gave her a gold watch; a relief fund reached nearly £1,000; and there were endless proposals of marriage. The first poem in her honour, eight rhetorical stanzas by an MP called Liddell, appeared on 20 October in the *Newcastle Journal*; it was followed by what can only be called effusions from William

Grace Darling

Wordsworth (poet laureate at the time), Swinburne and William McGonagall – with little to choose between them in poetic merit.

Grace herself was little affected by it all. William Howitt, a local poet, described her as 'neither tall nor handsome; but she has the most gentle, quiet, aimiable look, and the sweetest smile that I ever saw in a person of her station and appearance.' Another spoke of her 'reserved and retiring disposition with a strong religious tendency of mind'. To a correspondent who urged her to get out and enjoy life she wrote soberly: 'Had you seen the awful wreck of the *Forfarshire*, the melancholy sight would have been more than sufficient to have driven the pleasures of this world out of your mind for ever.' She made it clear to all that she did not want to marry while her parents were alive. In fact, she developed consumption a few years later and died of it in 1842, in the same Bamburgh bed where she had been born, the seventh child of a seventh child, 26 years before. She is buried in Bamburgh churchyard, a hundred yards away.

After Grace's death her elder sister Thomasin lived on Longstone to look after her parents. In 1841 a second house was built on Longstone to accommodate William Brooks Darling, his wife and family; it was his elder brother, William Darling, who succeeded his father as keeper when the latter was finally pensioned off (on full pay) in 1860. Her father outlived Grace by 33 years and is also buried in Bamburgh.

The Grace Darling story has been of lasting and incalculable benefit in stirring the imaginations of young and old, and in keeping public attention focused on the unending work of the Royal National Lifeboat Institution and other such beneficent organisations. The Bamburgh village Museum, started in the 1930s, now attracts some 50,000 visitors a year. It shows a typical Northumberland coble named *Grace Darling* – it is most unlikely to be the original one, since most of that seems to have been chopped up for souvenir hunters in 1838 – but the coble is vivid and actual enough to bring to life again for us all the events of that disastrous morning 150 years ago.

11

A Victorian in the Arctic

It began as a shooting trip 'with my friend Mr Mervyn Powys'. Quite normal in 1894, apparently, for two Englishmen to charter a 90-foot schooner-rigged steam yacht in Glasgow and breeze off into the Arctic Ocean for a holiday. Mr Powys was 'glad of the opportunity of sport in those regions'; his partner, Aubyn Trevor-Battye, the hero of this narrative, an amateur explorer and naturalist, already experienced in northern Canada, went out of mere curiosity to visit the quite large, but harbourless and unapproachable island of Kolguev. It is perhaps hardly surprising to learn that Trevor-Battye is still the last West European known to have spent three months on this or any other island in the Arctic Ocean – probably he was the first as well as the last; but the fact that he spent his time there by accident makes his story all the more remarkable.

Dark, dapper, humorous, rather military in mien, with a straight upper lip under his bushy black moustache, the face looking out at us from under its sealskin cap in the frontispiece to one of his books gives us some idea of what to expect from Trevor-Battye in emergency, but hardly prepares us for the vast range of assorted scientific knowledge he had at his fingertips – an intellectual equipment which the gentlemen explorers of his age evidently took more or less for granted.

The S.Y. *Saxon*, 117 tons, built of wood sheathed with copper, drawing 12 ft., and crewed by Scottish whaling men, left Peterhead on 2 June, via Bergen and Tromsö, round the North Cape to Vardö, their last port on Norwegian soil, where

Aubyn Trevor-Battye

they spent a few days bird-watching with the British Consul
on offshore islands.

By 15 June they were at anchor off Kolguev – flat, forlorn,
uninviting, yet with all the allure of the unknown. The *Saxon*'s
crew found the whole venture most puzzling, quite unlike the
'gentlemen's yachting' they had always heard about, yet with
no prospect of the kind of sport they might have enjoyed
themselves – not a whale or a bear in sight. Trevor-Battye kept
reading to them in the cabin during the evenings from the only
two accounts of Kolguev known to him, one of which made no
bones about its coasts being 'extremely dangerous on account
of the slight depth of the sea and the sandbanks'. It was thus
almost a direct answer to their misgivings that this year of all
years the jagged, hummocky, greenish pack ice was still, two
months later than normal, found to be drifting down from the
Pole into these waters. *Saxon* had to keep moving continuously
day and night to avoid being iced up; their various trial
landings could only be of a few hours each; and Powys soon
convinced himself that the sport on Novaya Zemblya, 200
miles away, was going to be much superior. Adding to the
general Old Testament gloom of the proceedings was an old
Greenland hand among the crew who all day cursed the
ice-floes at the top of his voice in fluent Gaelic as he fended
them off the hull.

After six days of to-ing and fro-ing in this tentative manner,
since Trevor-Battye showed no sign of listening to reason or of
being deflected in any way from his objective, a British
compromise was reached. It was decided that Trevor-Battye
and Hyland – a large, rather lethargic Wiltshire greengrocer
he had brought with him to help stuff the bird specimens –
should go ashore, with Sailor their spaniel, and strike east
across the island to make contact if possible with the
Samoyeds which were thought, but not known, to live there.
Meanwhile *Saxon* would extricate herself and return with
Powys to Vardö, from which she would set out again to pick
up the Kolguev party when the ice conditions allowed. Saying
their good-byes, the crew made it clear they never expected to
see Trevor-Battye or Hyland again; indeed they never did,
since though *Saxon* returned in August and a landing party

found one of Trevor-Battye's messages, ice and fog were still too bad for them to stay and make proper contact, and they were back home in Peterhead by 21 August.

When it became known in Archangel that there were two Englishmen marooned on Kolguev, the local British Consul started out to help, as did two intrepid British ladies, Mrs Leybourne Popham and Mrs Ponsonby, who set off from Vardö in S.Y. *Blencathra* in a rescue attempt, but were beaten back by storms. The Royal Geographical Society in London opened a subscription list, and Trevor-Battye's brother – who somewhat confuses the dramatis personae by electing to be known as Captain Trevor Battye-Trevor – came up to London to plan a relief expedition. Meanwhile the Foreign Office opened a file on the subject, this including a minute from that noted amateur ornithologist Sir Edward Grey, later Earl Grey of Fallodon, but at that time only an under-secretary: he took a personal interest as soon as he learned that one of Trevor-Battye's aims was to locate the nesting-place of the curlew-sandpiper. The Russian authorities, when approached in St Petersburg, had to admit they were helpless, since the few traders' flat-bottomed boats which did visit Kolguev could only do so at the end of the summer each year. In fact, in spite of all the outer world could do, Trevor-Battye and Hyland remained on Kolguev from 22 June to 18 September.

They camped for their first two nights at the mouth of the Gusina river where they had been put ashore, near the northern tip of the island. Their first day was fine, 62° in the sun, and they spent it shooting for the pot and packing their stores, which included dried apple chips, methylated spirits, Liebig's extract, quinine pills and essence of ginger; together with a gun and 250 cartridges their load came to over 50 lb each. In addition Trevor-Battye carried a telescope, revolver, pocket microscope, watch, money, tooth-powder and brush; and Hyland a kettle tied round his waist with string. When they had finished laughing at each other in their funny get-up, they set off to walk across the central plateau of the island towards the harbour of Scharok on the south-east coast.

Some days they suffered from heat and mosquitoes, their hands and ears swelled up, and they found that mirage effects

are as much a feature of arctic as of sandy deserts. A good deal
of their navigation was by sheer hunch, and it was not till 3
a.m. on the morning of June 29th that they came on their first
inhabited Samoyed *choom*. Here with the aid of a little whisky
and a little bad Russian, the only common language, friendly
relations were quickly established with Uano and his family,
who cooked them a goose on the spot. (How many of us would
do as much for two strangers knocking us up at 3 a.m.?) After
Trevor-Battye had returned the kindness by brewing cocoa
and letting them smoke his pipe, they all turned in. Contact
had been duly made with the most northerly settlement of the
57 Samoyeds who lived on Kolguev, and who were destined to
be their hosts for another three months.

A SAMOYED SHOOTING REINDEER
The man is screened behind a lump of turf in which reindeer horns are fixed as a decoy

(*Drawn by Onaska, on Kolguev*)

Stocky, bowlegged and Mongolian in appearance, Samoyeds are the remains of the primitive tribes which lived in the
Urals and Altai mountains of Central Russia, and have since
become widely scattered all over Siberia and Arctic Russia,
leading a nomadic existence mainly as reindeer-farmers. Little
is still known about them since their numbers are thought not
to exceed 25,000 in all; but their language belongs to the small
group which includes Finnish and Hungarian, their religion is
shamanic, and they have retained unusual sophistication in
their cooking pots, cutlery and other domestic metalwork.
Trevor-Battye notes how many of their names are corruptions
of Biblical ones: On Tipa (Antipas), Yelisei (Elisha), Onaska
(Ananias) and so on. Carlyle speaks of Samoyeds as examples
of legendary barbarity, and the Russian word *samo-yedi*

certainly means 'a self-eater'; but when Trevor-Battye taxed one of their old men with this taste for cannibalism, he was answered with a dry smile. 'Yes, but not now.' There are a few learned works by Russian and German anthropologists dealing with Samoyed culture; but it is doubtful if many others from the outside world have ever been so wholeheartedly welcomed into the homes and the daily life of a Samoyed tribe as these two passing English sportsmen were in the summer of 1894.

It was not all plain sailing. At their first encounter Trevor-Battye had brandished rather too freely a handsome red-sealed *laisser-passer* issued to him the year before by the governor of Archangel; so his hosts, reasonably enough, got it into their heads that here were the governor's personal emissaries, and that when they returned with them the next day to the north of the island they would find the governor standing there in person, or at the worst a high-level shipwreck which would lend itself to looting. When they found only the Englishmen's tiny green canvas tent, they were much disappointed; but the wonders that began to emerge from this modest treasury went far to reassure them – a sharp, shining English axe, several sides of salt pork, tea, dried figs and a bird-identification book with coloured plates – and their natural hospitality did the rest. Sailor the spaniel played his part too in giving demonstrations of retrieving game, a feat which astounded them all. Through the weeks which followed, the two Englishmen so endeared themselves to their hosts that the latter ended by making every offer in their power to get them to stay on through the winter; but even their trump card, the promise of a bear shoot by full moonlight, somehow failed to take the trick.

In the middle of July Trevor-Battye thought it best to move away from Uano's *choom* down to Scharok harbour (known today as Bugrino), where they expected *Saxon* to put in when she returned, or where they were most likely to find some other craft to take them off. The only harbour and the principal inhabited place on the island – which was not saying much – Scharok consisted of little but a few locked wooden huts, a disused church, a cemetery and several mounds of old

reindeer bones, the whole subject to the permanent defect of
all Arctic settlements, that the ground was everywhere thick
and slippery with many years' accumulation of seal fat. One of
the wooden huts was put at their disposal. For Hyland it was
mainly a sick-bay: he felt the cold continuously, got giddy
after even small exertions, and spent many of his days lying in
his sleeping-bag complaining of severe pains across the small
of the back. Trevor-Battye, who evidently felt some remorse at
having tempted the Wiltshireman away from his quiet country
life to come on the expedition at all, was no less diligent in the
role of doctor and nurse than he was as ornithologist and
surveyor.

The Scharok days passed in the usual small change of
camping – fetching water, shooting for the pot and gathering
driftwood for fires. The Samoyeds gave them constant tea and
vodka parties (though all Hyland wanted was beer), these
evenings ending in song and dance and endless games of
draughts at which Trevor-Battye gave universal pleasure by
always getting beaten. He learned all the reindeer lore and
practice they could teach him, including the use of the lassoo
(*di-zha*); but they couldn't join quite as fervently as expected
in the occasional family banquets on raw reindeer meat –
Samoyeds regard the windpipe as the greatest delicacy. There
were bow and arrow contests, wood-whittling and doll-
carving for the children, and English lessons – all this in
addition to the systematic botany and ornithology which were
Trevor-Battye's reason for being there at all. And one day
they sent for him to join them on a 'goosing'.

Richard Finch, an English trader who paid a casual visit to
'Colguieue' in 1611 wrote that 'the Russes' were in the habit
of netting geese there in quantity 'before they bee ouer fledge'.
In 1894, nearly 300 years later, they were still at it; one of the
most important events of the Samoyed year, the goosings still
provided the islanders with their main store of food for the
winter and with a useful export. In the manner of an English
farm harvest, it was at the same time both a working occasion
and a social festival; made more memorable for them this year
by the presence of their strange English guest, who all the way
to the goosing ground kept studying his compass, stopping to

SAMOYED SHOOTING FOXES IN WINTER

(Drawn by Onaska, on Kolguev)

peer through his telescope and sitting down to make sketches of the flowers.

They first trained him in the use of the *parlka*, an iron-toothed truncheon for hurling at the birds to bring them down as they took flight, and then set to, in five rowboats, driving the feeding geese across the tidal flats and crowding them into a huge circular net stockade some forty yards across. In fact the great majority were moulting brent geese which neither took flight nor dived but, after a moment's awkward hesitation, followed the first of their number up the bank and packed themselves into the net, a dense black heaving mass, without a single one breaking away. The killing was a long and tedious business: each bird had to be picked up by the head and whirled quickly round to dislocate its neck. At the end of the day – and it was a most exceptional day, never repeated that summer – the count was 3,300 brent, 13 bean geese and 12 white-fronted; and 40 of this magnificent bag were presented ceremonially to Trevor-Battye – five of the Samoyeds came up and each in turn gave him eight geese with the same little speech of thanks. Some days later they returned to the creek to store the geese in clamps under the turf until they were ready later still, working again as a family outing, to skin them and salt them away in barrels for the winter. There were 300 to each barrel, the value of each barrel traded to the Russians being two roubles.

The boat that was eventually to take them off arrived on August 17th, the only boat regularly visiting Kolguev from the outer world, and that only once a year. It was a sailing ketch operated by a Russian trader, Alexander Samarakov, and was the last but one of a much bigger fleet which had plied regularly to Kolguev fifty years before; since those days a plague had decimated the island's reindeer population and

SAMOYEDS KILLING WALRUS
The black dots on the right are heads of seals at which a man, lying on the ice, shoots

(*Drawn by Onaska, on Kolguev*)

reduced to nothing the island's importance in the Russian scheme of things. Samarakov's stock-in-trade was mainly cotton goods, salt fish, snuff, tea and sugar, and his business, now that there was no longer any competition, was a good one, requiring a whole month to discharge. He had the help of his factotum Yakov, a swashbuckling ex-soldier who was regarded with universal reverence because he had once been as far away as St Petersburg. His hold crammed with salted goose and reindeer meat, Samarakov finally set sail for the mainland with his two English passengers and their dog on September 18th, when the ground was already covered again with the first of the winter's snow. They made landfall with some difficulty twenty hours later off Okshin at the mouth of the Pechora river.

A SAMOYED TAKING A DEER WITH THE DI-ZHA

(*Drawn by Onaska, on Kolguev*)

The Englishmen's onward journey was successfully accomplished in the face of a series of further difficulties, chief among which was the fact that their passage up the Pechora and their subsequent crossing of 1,000 miles of North Russian tundra fell to be performed at the very time of year which

Russians themselves, after centuries of experience, regard as
unthinkable for any kind of travel at all. In the season known
to Russians as *rasputye*, corresponding roughly to the month of
October, the dry of summer has not yet given place to the dry
snow and solid ice of winter: it freezes one day and thaws the
next, so that the whole land is a morass of mud, and the rivers,
charged with heavy floating lumps of ice, are extremely
hazardous for boats. Five reindeer have to be harnessed to
each sleigh, in place of the two normal at all other times of
year; this is not merely to give better traction across the
surface slime, but so that, when one reindeer subsides
suddenly up to its neck in a hidden pool of mud, the rest can
be deployed all round to haul it out. During this travellers'
off-season even the official Russian mail service came to an
end and all postmen regarded themselves as on holiday; all
labour contracts were off, and the statutory obligation on
innkeepers to provide a change of horses for travellers was also
in abeyance.

This *rasputye* season beat Napoleon, and after him Hitler,
but it didn't beat Trevor-Battye. 'Mad dogs and Englishmen'
go out in the autumn swamps. The reason for pushing on
regardless was in part ordinary cussedness, in part shortage of
money, and in part the promise he had given his companion to
be home in good time for Christmas, so that Hyland would
not miss the best trading weeks of the greengrocer's year. In
fact Hyland was still feeling the cold badly and spending a
great part of the day fast asleep in the various sleighs,
tarantasses and other vehicles provided for transporting the
expedition, so could do little himself to help things forward.
The brunt fell on Trevor-Battye, who by a mixture of personal
charm, ingenious improvisations, early rising, force of
example, haggling, strenuous physical labour and the calm
reiteration at every crisis of the formula 'I am going on'
triumphantly scolded and cajoled his little party without a
single casualty human or animal across eight or nine large
rivers and a thousand miles of tundra to the nearest
considerable outpost of civilisation, Archangel.

Three minor Russian habits annoyed him as much as any of
the major hardships of the journey. One was the reliance of

many of the men on vodka, which often removed one of them
from circulation altogether just at the moment he was wanted;
a second was the practice they had, when anything unpopular
was suggested, of quietly disappearing into the surrounding
forest, out of which they would reappear only in the evening,
in time for supper but too late to do what had been proposed;
a third was the constant desire of Russian officials to kiss his
hand. 'It is meant well', he writes severely, 'but it is irritating,
and opposed to our ideas.'

The party stayed for a few days in Askinö, trader
Samarakov's village, and on 4 October set forth on their
journey up the broad, flooded Pechora to Ust Tsilma in a long
narrow trading boat rowed by three oarsmen. Here they
borrowed a hundred roubles from the local chief of police
(*ispravnik*) 'on note of hand only' and started in horse-drawn
sleighs on their crossing of the tundra. This is the treeless,
swampy waste several hundred miles deep that extends along
the 4,000 miles of the shores of the Arctic Ocean. The track of
sorts that is reasonably well defined in summer and winter
vanishes into the mud during *rasputye*; so that though there
were 39 staging posts between Ust Tsilma and Archangel the
business of navigating from one to another presented
problems of its own, in addition to the difficulty of getting any
action out of the staging posts in the slack season.

Against these minor irritations two things played an
unexpectedly useful part: one, the old spaniel Sailor, whose
long silky ears were irresistible to the village women
everywhere, and whose demonstrations of retrieving continued to astonish both Russians and Samoyeds alike and to
fortify their respect for the wisdom and importance of his
master. Allied to this was Trevor-Battye's foresight in arming
himself, in Archangel the year before, with two sets of official
papers hung about with large red state seals, requiring
preferential treatment for 'a member of the Linnean and
Zoological Society of London, A. Trevor-Battye' everywhere
before other travellers. Even in places where the local officials
couldn't read, the swinging red seals did their work; and
discreet use could be made of the word 'governor' – for
example, shouted vaguely across a river at dusk, this often

produced a boat from the other side with surprisingly little delay.

They made Archangel by the end of October. Here Hyland recovered at once on eating green vegetables and finding some letters from his sweetheart awaiting him; and the only two resident Englishmen among the town's 17,000 inhabitants, the British Consul and the owner of a sawmill, killed the fatted calf for the travellers in no uncertain fashion. On November 5th they left again by sleigh, and as the ground was now properly frozen made good time to the railhead at Vologda on November 10th. And so via Yaroslavl, Moscow, St. Petersburg, through Germany home – in good time for Hyland's Christmas trade in Marlborough.

It was not quite an end of the matter. Owing to the absence of communications in the area, the efforts, British and Russian, to organize a rescue were carried on long after Trevor-Battye had reached the mainland, and were finally called off only on 28 October when he and Hyland presented themselves in Archangel, from which the British Consul could telegraph the news to the outer world. In March 1895 the Foreign Office, ever vigilant about its expenditure as all government departments should be, sent in a bill for their trouble to Trevor-Battye – £32 4s for the various sorties of Mr Henry Cooke, H.M. Vice Consul in Archangel, and £12 14s 9d for the necessary official telegrams between London and St. Petersburg.

Like a true Englishman Trevor-Battye refused to pay, mainly on the ground that he had never asked to be rescued, since he had told Powys exactly what he intended to do, and had done it; also that Cooke's attempt to land on Kolguev had been a minimal departure from the routine of his official summer touring duties anyway. After some cold correspondence in tones of nicely barbed courtesy on both sides, the Foreign Secretary, the Earl of Kimberley, intervened personally, advising that the sum of £44 18s 9d might properly be charged to public funds, to which the Treasury agreed. Trevor-Battye had got his way once more.

12

3,400 Miles in Open Boats

The carriage in British ships of chemically dangerous or unstable cargoes is rightly hedged about today with every possible kind of restriction, at the instance of both marine insurers and of those responsible for the safety and working conditions of seamen. Among such cargoes can certainly be classed the metal concentrates or 'slimes' habitually shipped during the 1920s from Australian mines to Europe for further metallurgical treatment. 'Slimes' gives a good picture of their nature and characteristics: they have the consistency of half-set cement, and are more or less impermeable to water.

Such was the sole cargo – 6,562 tons of zinc slimes – which SS *Trevessa* loaded at Port Pirie, South Australia, in May 1923. The ship, of 5,000 tons gross, owned and operated by the Hain Steamship Co. of St Ives, Cornwall, was a vessel with a chequered history. Built in Flensburg in 1909 as the *Imkenturm* for German owners, she had spent most of World War One interned in tropical waters in Sourabaya, Dutch East Indies. Handed over as reparations after the war, with her hull corroded after years of idleness, she was brought to England in 1919 for repair, and received her A1 100 certificate in 1921. Part of the refit was the substitution of six British-built wooden lifeboats for the original German metal ones. As she passed through a hurricane on her first Atlantic crossing she was reported as 'behaving magnificently'. This was the vessel – squat, dumpy, with one slender funnel – which joined two others from the same company, SS *Trevean* and *Tregenna* at Port Pirie to embark their cargoes for Europe.

It was established at courts of enquiry later that neither the nature nor the bulk of the *Trevessa*'s cargo was anything out of the ordinary, and that the concentrates had been loaded in a routine manner under the supervision of a strict port superintendent of many years' experience. After coaling up in Fremantle, Western Australia, they set sail for Antwerp, via Durban, on 25 May.

Eleven days later, crossing the south of the Indian Ocean, they ran into a violent storm with Force 7-9 gales, in the course of which the crew, from their fo'c'sle quarters, heard water beginning to swish about in No. 1 forward hold; from here owing to the nature of the slime covering the floor of the hold the water had no chance to run away down into the bilges, from which it would have been extracted in the normal way by the pumps, all of which were working perfectly. The ship rapidly began to settle by the head, and at 1.0 a.m. on 4 June all hands were ordered into No. 1 and No. 3 starboard lifeboats – the other two main lifeboats having been damaged in the storm the day before. Ship was abandoned at 2.15 a.m., and she foundered, standing almost on end with all lights burning, at 2.45, watched by her crew in their boats.

The ship's black cat was put in one of the boats, but jumped back aboard and went down with the ship. Captain Foster, who was curious about such things, noted this as the climax of his ship's unfortunate 'cat history'. This began with the first ship's cat deserting in Timaru, New Zealand, on the way out; a second black cat adopted in Port Pirie deserted before sailing; later still a fine tabby in the crew's quarters aboard died between Port Pirie and Fremantle before giving birth to her kittens – to the disgust of the crew who had organised a sweep among themselves on the number of kittens she would have.

So there they were, the whole complement of officers and men, in their two lifeboats, 1640 miles out from Fremantle, about 1730 miles south east of Mauritius, at a point in the Indian Ocean just about as far from land as it is possible to be anywhere in the world. The distribution in the boats by nationality was as follows:

	No. 1 *Capt C.P.T. Foster*	No. 3 *1st Officer J.C.S. Smith*
English	6	13
Scots	2	2
Irish	3	2
Welsh	2	1
Swedish	–	1
Burmese	2	1
Arab	2	–
Portuguese African	2	–
Indian	1	4
Afghan	–	1
	20	25

Each boat was 26 feet long, 8 foot 3 at maximum width. The seating arrangements – huddling arrangements would be a better word – were the same in each boat; carpenters and seamen up forward round the mast, native firemen and others amidships, officers, engineers and steward aft at the tiller. At the start the boats sailed in touch with each other, but after a week it was decided that as No. 1 carried a bigger spread of sail than No. 3 it was better to separate. Not that the larger sail was always an asset; it had constantly to be furled and goose-winged to take account of storms and a weakness in the mast mounting. Both skippers kept logs of their daily progress, and Capt Foster had managed to bring with him all the crew's paybooks and other records.

Of prime importance in the days which followed was the manner in which the two lifeboats had been victualled during the last hectic hour aboard. Foster had himself been twice torpedoed within 16 hours during World War One, and had learned from his nine days in an open boat that weight for weight condensed milk is far more sustaining than meat products, also that tobacco and cigarettes played an essential part in maintaining morale. The boats of course already carried their standard rations of ship's biscuit and water in screw-top breakers, as required by the Board of Trade regulations. The difficulty of manhandling the provision cases from the after store room across a tilting slippery deck at the height of the storm needs no emphasis; but they were minimised by the fact that the young chief steward had sailed for five years with Foster and had been well briefed by him in advance of the emergency. A last-minute inspiration of Foster's, to toss a leather suitcase full of clothes into the boat, paid unexpected dividends later, strips of the cut-up leather being particularly useful for various mechanical improvisations.

At all times the basic liquid rations of milk (four tablespoonsful per man per day) and water (three tablespoonsful) were scrupulously maintained, and supplemented by whatever extra water could be collected during rain squalls by day or night. So great was the benefit of water to both health and morale of all concerned – so much greater indeed the need for water than for the ration of biscuits and other foods which were often too dry to be swallowed, or even chewed – that during all rain squalls it became their habit to lower sail and concentrate on collecting the water by every ingenious device they could think of. These included beating out a biscuit tin into a sort of bib which went under their chins so that they could squeeze out the rain that fell on their hair and beards – the bib leading down into a second tin held against the chest to collect the water. Another method was for a sailor to stand back to the storm in his oilskin, the lower hem of which was folded over into a sloping gutter delivering the rain into another tin. Water wrung out of the canvas boat cover under which they crouched at night was too often found to be brackish from the salt impregnating the cover.

Putting their heads and necks over the side of the boat and getting a second man to sluice sea water over them was a useful cooling method in the tropical heat of midday; and Foster taught them from his own experience the benefit of sniffing sea water up the nostrils and spitting it out again at once. Anyone unable to hold back from swallowing sea water, even from damping biscuits in it, paid for it with severe stomach pains, and in two cases with death. Severe stomach pains were also the reward of one crew member undisciplined enough to take covert swigs at the spirit in the compass mounting, and at the ship's small supply of storm oil.

Captain Foster's seamanship was matched by his understanding of his men as individuals, the strong and weak points of each. He made great play with his daily ritual readings of the sextant, which some of the men clearly thought was a magical apparatus; each day after reading it he was careful to smile cheerfully and exhibit to all a confidence about their progress he often knew he had no reason whatever to feel. And so, telling stories, with the occasional singsong, rowing short distances when they found the strength to do so, comparing notes about the different makes of ship's biscuit, massaging their feet with storm oil to promote circulation, and baling continuously they carried on their way as cheerfully as might be, and finally found themselves in the path of the S.E. trade winds which helped them to make better progress. Their heroism was of the most difficult kind, displayed in cold blood with the whole day and night in which to brood about their misfortunes, if they so wished.

It was the carpenter in No. 1 boat who first saw land, thus earning the extra water ration that Foster had promised to the first man to do so; it was on the afternoon of 26 June, their 23rd day in the boat. Though they had been steering for Mauritius, and at the same time prudently holding enough rations in hand to carry them on to Madagascar if they missed Mauritius, it was in fact the island of Rodriguez, 344 miles east of Mauritius, that they saw, and were able with the help of a local fisherman to find one of the two openings in the coral reef surrounding it. Rodriguez, an outstation of the Eastern Telegraph Co. on the line of the cable from Durban to West Australia, was an island of 7000 inhabitants, overseen by one magistrate, one priest and one doctor. At Port Mathurin, their largest settlement, the islanders gave the *Trevessa* men as riotous a welcome as their modest resources, medical and domestic, would permit – the crewmen's first hot cup of tea for more than three weeks being the greatest success of all. Four days later a RN destroyer HMS *Colombo* arrived to take them on to Mauritius. Of some interest is the fact that though they one and all looked forward to a long deep sleep as the climax of their adventures, this was denied to them: their first night ashore they felt no inclination but to sit up talking till all hours.

Meanwhile on the 28th No. 3 boat reached Mauritius, where they too were guided in through the reef by local fishermen. Considerably more crowded than No. 1, they had lost eight out of their complement of 25, and another man, the ship's cook, died in hospital after landing: No. 1 had lost only two out of their complement, both Arabs. What had been a riotous welcome on Rodriguez turned into a civic carnival in Mauritius when the two boat crews were reunited and more sophisticated hospitals had helped them all to recover their strength. Each crew member on recovery was welcomed into a local home and treated as one of the family. A welfare fund was organized, and on July 11th there was a full-scale thanksgiving service in the Port Louis cathedral, after which Captain Foster presented each crew member to the Governor. The next day there was a preliminary enquiry.

On 16 July they left for England in RMS *Goorkha* of the Union Castle line via Durban, where – to his complete surprise, for he was the most modest of men – they united to present Captain Foster with a gold cigarette case for which they had all subscribed. By the end of August they were back in England, where Captain and Mrs Foster were received by King George V. The Board of Trade ceremonially presented him with a silver tea service, and Mr Smith, skipper of No. 3 boat, with a silver inkstand. The No. 1 boat had been purchased in Mauritius by a local company, which later sent it over to London for exhibition at the 1924 Wembley Exhibition.

The official enquiry by the Board of Trade Wreck Commissioner took place in London on November 15th, without being able to assign any definite cause for the leak in the *Trevessa*. The enquiry concluded:

> The Court is unable to find words adequately to express its members' admiration for the fine seamanship and resolution of the officers, the splendid discipline and courage of the crew, both European and non-European. The Court desires to express deep sympathy with the relatives of those who lost their lives.

13

An Italian in the Red Sea

The following is an extract translated from the diary of one of the officers of the Italian submarine Macalle *which was left behind by him on the islet of Barr Musa Kebir in the Red Sea on which he was castaway after the loss of his ship on 15 June 1940. In places the writing is illegible. The author was plainly suffering acutely – on a sunstruck rock in the Red Sea in June – from his hardships, the lack of food and the bad quality of the meagre ration of water.*

After having charged our batteries and cleaned the accumulators as well as possible we continued on our course. The sea is rough and we feel sick when on the surface. Twice I suffered from cramp in the stomach, and throughout the day I have had severe gripes. Last night we arrived at our ordered position.

To-morrow we start our patrol. There is no improvement in the condition of foodstuffs, only cold food as standard menu ... only milk in the mornings, which although cold is the best nourishment.

June 13 – Thursday
We dive at dawn. Same as yesterday. Slow speed while submerged – from time to time at periscope-depth, in order to explore the area. Most of the crew stationed forward are sick, we don't know what causes this or why we have fever and pains and fits of vomiting and cramp. I was there this morning to check one of the motors, a real disaster, dirty and messy, an exceptional stink. Last night it was rough and some of them

suffered, so that there was vomit and excrement in the ...(?) I believe that most of them were affected by each other. In the after section we are all well, I have had constipation, and since I left I have not been able to use the w.c., but under the new system I don't even give it a thought. This evening we expect rough weather again – we are at about 20 metres depth and rolling just as if we were on the surface. We shall surface in about an hour's time. The temperature is about 39 degrees, 102·2 Fahrenheit – breathing is heavy.

We surfaced at 1915 in a rough sea which makes us roll. Having started up the engines and begun to charge the batteries, I went to stretch myself aft, in the hope of being able to rest, but it was impossible. The bunk was moving to such an extent that I had to lash it. At midnight I got up very drowsy; after ten minutes I went on watch. I was very sick, after which I felt better. I ... and smoked a cigarette – the first of the day. I returned to my post and felt frightfully sleepy. I could barely hold out until four o'clock when I was relieved. My thoughts were at home and I can scarcely wait for the time to return in order to obtain some news.

June 14 – Friday
We dived at the usual hour, at about seven. A loud crash forward, but I do not know what this comes from.

About midday I find out that the whole crew aft is in a very bad state. We fear that this is due to some escape of chlorine from the air-conditioning-compressors. The effect of this gas makes them vomit and they all seem dead-drunk. They cannot utter one word and make odd noises. About fifty have been affected by this, and amongst them one more severely than the rest, *i.e.*, the Torpedo Petty Officer, who can barely stand on his feet. We have remained submerged a long time and the air-consumption has been heavy: to-night we will have to charge up for some time. I went to rest at 2030, but I was not sleepy. There was no means of going to sleep. I relieved the watch at midnight and after a time the starboard motor makes a strange noise and some parts come loose. We stop the engine in order to make the necessary repairs – this at 0215, not exact time, but approximate. We start up the engines again to finish charging.

I examine thoroughly the working of the flooding-valves (?) and was about to check the intensity of the charge, when I felt a heavy bump, the whole boat shook excessively within the space of a few seconds; a series of thumps and I felt the submarine reel under the blows. An ambush. In no time the submarine heels over to 90° to port. The ... which I was holding in front of me now serve as ... The crew, who were sleeping at their posts with the exception of the watch, get up and in their eyes I can see loss of control.

To put an end to our queries, we hear the voices of the Captain, who communicates through the speaking-tube with the second-in-command, who is stationed in the interior of the submarine. I remain aft, trying to keep the crew calm. But they are shaken and it is difficult to understand what has happened. But what we do know is that we are on the surface or at least at a few metres from it. We prepare the rescue diving-gear, they are insufficient in number for the complement aft. The collision-doors are open and you can see right through to the Control-Room, where one can see a crowd of men without knowing what they are doing. The speaking-tube from the Control-Room informs us that we are on the surface and (orders us) to remain calm at our diving-stations.

I reply that it is necessary to send somebody to close the seacocks because I see water in great quantities pouring into the pumping engines, so much so that I fear that the water is penetrating into the auxiliary room and consequently into the after batteries. I see a stoker closing some valves; a Petty Officer Electrician coming aft gives me some details of the situation.

Some of the crew are already on deck and others are going there. Subsequently I find out that one of the after batteries is giving out smoke or steam without being able to smell the chlorine which is in small quantities.

Having heard this I go to explore the position and to see how things stand. I give orders to the crew to remain at their posts and that I will tell them what is to be done.

At 0245 I go to the Control-Room, the crew continues to leave it in couples, using the rescue-hatch. These operations are directed by the Chief Engineer. The crew continues to leave, and I help two Petty Officer Electricians to leave the Control-Room, after which I insist that the crew aft leaves to come to the Control-Room. I order them to abandon the stern and come to the Control-Room. The same thing in the bows. I find myself at a moment in which no one is ready to go up and I go up with the first of those in the bows.

On deck I see the *Macalle* on her port side. I feel sure that she will never put to sea again.

From the building slips to such an end ...

June 15 – *Saturday.*
On deck a quick roll call is held, including the many who are injured, and it was not easy to get them on deck.

We start work on salvaging the foodstuffs and other articles. The deck is practically full. Owing to low-tide the boat is inclined to heel more and more, which makes it advisable to suspend action and send everything on shore. In the meantime the dinghy is lowered for the transport ashore of provisions and members of the crew.

I dive into the sea and swim to the shore. The distance is not very great and with four strokes I touch bottom.

The bottom is rocky. I landed ashore after falling several times and grazing my leg, which I had already knocked when we ran aground. The first streaks of daylight can be seen and we can clearly see our plight. The submarine is listing to such an extent that it is not possible to open the hatches without letting in water.

We continue to try to recover provisions, but the escape of chlorine is very strong ...

One cannot do more! Some of the respirators are recovered, but even these are ill-adapted for our particular need.

Ashore we check the stores. I believe that there are 53 bottles of liquor and Ailet mineral-water, two cases of biscuits, a tin of bacon, three tins of jam, all we have. Ashore there are 45 of us in good health.

All we have is less than what we normally consume at one sitting.

I make a tour of the island to find out where I am. The

whole area does not exceed 500 square metres, there is a strong wind, and the island is in part covered with sand and in part with scrub.

Where we landed there is a signpost with 'INTREP ...' We find some stones laid with a certain regularity; one can see that in 1936 there was an expedition to take topographical bearings.

The island is completely deserted.

I return on board in the hopes of being able to make myself useful, but as I see nothing can be done, we make plans and nothing else. I return to the shore and lie in the water. I was sleepy but I cannot rest.

I return on board for another attempt to get below, but this time also I am obliged to give it up. Up to a little while ago I had heard some machinery still running, but then nothing further, and according to what I was told by the last man to go inside the submarine, there was no more light, the batteries were run down through some leakage.

A last party goes on board at about 1700 to make a final effort to recover provisions from the food part of the submarine, by attempting to flood one of the compartments aft.

Having opened the hatch, little water enters and only enters after a rush of air-bubbles; this means that the interior is completely flooded, leaving only an air-pocket which is gradually disappearing.

The crew is leaving with the dinghy ... The boat slowly lifts her bows, then with increasing speed slides backwards, levels up almost vertically and disappears. My old *Macalle*, in which I have spent nearly three-and-a-half years, has ceased to exist; but before leaving us she has left us on a rock and safe. After she disappears, we see nothing for several seconds, then later a large patch of oil and then the engine-room telegraph gives us its last salute in the shape of ... Something else is seen in the distance and everything follows the current and rapidly drifts away. It is 1730. The submarine has ceased to exist; inglorious ending if you like, but she has set free every man of her crew.

On shore we work with alacrity, we are facing the only hope which is left to us, to send some sort of message to ask for help.

We are about 30 miles away from Port Sudan, an Anglo-Egyptian port. If help comes from there it means that we will be interned in a concentration-camp. The Captain decides to try for the Eritrean coast, which lies fifty miles beyond.

The departure, which had been fixed for the next morning, is put forward to to-night. We all rush to make ourselves useful and the expedition is fitted out with all the means at our disposal, provisions, compass, sail, electric torch, in fact, all that can be found on this sunburnt soil.

At 2135 the expedition leaves under favourable conditions; the wind is favourable and the sea is calm. The expedition is under the command of a midshipman and is composed of three men in all, the ... one seaman – a real bull – and a midshipman. Our destiny depends on them. Good wishes are not sufficient. We return to our hideout, made of scrub and boards, but it protects us from the wind. After such a heavy day we did not see food, only a spoonful of water in a glass, this is all for to-day and I am going to rest.

June 16 – *Sunday*
I slept like the dead, a heavy sleep. As soon as I woke up, I made an attempt to distill some water but I did not succeed. I tried by means of two bottles and also by means of a filter, but I was unable to obtain even a drop.

I wandered like a ... in the hopes of finding food. Hunger has made its appearance, which was not felt yesterday. I find some very small shell-fish, which I ate; the stuff increased my thirst, as it was salty.

At midday the lunch consisted of one shell-fish a head, a real Sunday.

What impresses me most are the sick men, three of these mention numbers and make strange remarks. One twists from one side to the other in search of water and they all have visions of eggs, fish and aeroplanes – to me it's like being in a madhouse, one of them is in a pitiful condition, thin as a rake, he rolls from side to side to the point of exhaustion and today he can hardly speak. His eyes are wide open, his lips are burned with thirst, and he hasn't the strength to keep on his feet. All these sick men are the despair of nearly all of us, nobody can bear the sight of them, and they all make fun of them. It breaks my heart. They are not ill through their own fault but through ... therefore they are being helped here although nothing can be done.

In the afternoon doing some experiments I fell into some hot water and burnt my stomach.

At 1900 we had our first meal from the provisions, one biscuit, one small plate of bacon, not more than 200 grammes, and a thimbleful of Ailet water, with a drop of brandy.

The roof of my mouth hurt me while eating. After this meal I succeeded in distilling some water but I only made a little, the production will be begun tomorrow. I went to rest at 1030.

June 17 – Monday
I slept heavily. I woke up. The first complaint from one of the sick men who was asking for a pal; he wants to speak to the Captain, saying that he is going to die either today or tomorrow.

He wishes to be buried with all Christian honours. This is today's greetings. A Petty Officer Electrician came, who yesterday drank some seawater and thought last night he was dying, as he had such cramp in the stomach, but today he is feeling better.

During the day I suffered very much from thirst, so much so that at one moment I thought my tongue was covered with fishscales and I could not move it. I have been looking out for the aeroplanes; according to my calculations our searchparty might have arrived today but in vain. I was a long time in the water, where one doesn't feel so thirsty, but it is terribly weakening. Getting out of the water last night, I was unable to walk at first; I walked with great difficulty, which gave me a shock. The meal at midday consisted of the usual shell-fish, which was alive and I had to pull off its legs, and I felt sorry, I had to kill it.

In the evening, biscuits with jam and a drop of water, this time not Ailet but distilled water made by my system and which gave good results. I believe that after one day, including the night, it will be possible to double the amount we are consuming at present.

After supper we were disillusioned by the sight of a ship, but I saw a light giving coloured signals, and in my excitement I mentioned it to the others, so much so that all of us saw the light, but it was not certain and we fired a rocket from the highest point of the island, but up to now nobody has been seen to come.

Tomorrow morning, I am on watch at the distilling-plant.

June 18 *Tuesday.*
The sick man is worse, whereas the others are improving.

I drank two seagull's eggs with Fernet Branca which has given me new strength. At midday another 'zabaglione' (usually yolk of egg beaten up in Marsala) with eggs, sugar, coffee, and a drop of Fernet. Found it very good and substantial.

Afternoon plans. Bathing.

To my disppointment I thought to find the usual biscuit with something, but nothing whatsoever. I felt ill.

Water has increased in quantity, but has depreciated in quality, and the distilled stuff, which smells of rubber, has been mixed with orangeade, but was not sufficiently diluted.

At 1530 and 1600 we heard some gunfire to the north; they say it was a good omen. The gunfire sounded more like a bombardment than a naval battle.

June 19 – *Wednesday*
We are still waiting. Waiting and wondering, but there is nothing.

Lunch to-day was seagulls *à la broche*. I could not eat them. I think it is due to stomach trouble.

At eight o'clock this morning I went into the water and having got a mouthful of salt water, I began to vomit, to such an extent that I became unconscious. When I came to, they had to carry me bodily ashore, and brought me to life with water and slapping my face.

As a second dish at lunchtime, a thimbleful of zabaglione like yesterday and a shell-fish. I couldn't digest the shell-fish, so that in the afternoon when I returned to the water I started to vomit again, but not so much.

At 0230 today the Torpedo Petty Officer died and has been released from his sufferings.

Life here is becoming unbearable. Swimming lessons ...

The story is continued from this point from reports received in the Admiralty and from an article in the Italian Press.

The six-foot dinghy with two oars and a makeshift sail in which the midshipman and two others started on June 15 in the faint hope of bringing help for the rest of the crew managed to reach Italian territory in Eritrea near Bas Kasar, nearly 100 miles away on the third day. From a frontier post they were able to send a message to Messawa.

Early on June 22 a British reconnaissance aircraft sighted the survivors from the Macalle *on the islet and a tug with an armed party was sent from Port Sudan to take them off. The tug arrived later in the morning but found that the survivors had already gone.*

In the interval, in the words of an Italian article 'What was the surprise of the crew when at dawn they saw advancing towards them the black hull of the rescuing submarine. In the distance and at first they thought it to be British and immediately prepared to sell their lives dear. Then as she gradually advanced she was recognized to be one of ours.'

This submarine took the survivors on board.

14

Four Broken Ribs

Mr. E.G. Elliott, a merchant seaman gunner, describes the loss of the British Umona, *3,767 tons, while bound from Walvis Bay for Freetown, and the almost incredible survival of one passenger and himself (with four broken ribs) after having spent thirteen days – five and a half of them without water – on a float five feet square with no protection from the tropical sun.*

Nothing of importance occurred until 2015 ATS on 30 March, when, in position 90 miles south of Freetown, we were torpedoed without warning on the starboard quarter. Nothing was seen of the submarine or the track of the torpedo; I was on the raised gun-platform over the poop, no water was thrown up, but the poop-deck was blown up, the gun rolled over to port, and I was flung from the platform to the well-deck. The explosion was fairly loud, but not so violent as might have been expected. It started a fire in the sailors' quarters probably caused by the steering engine blowing up and setting light to the surplus oil. We could not deal with this fire as the hoses and pipe-lines were smashed to pieces.

I do not know what happened to the rest of the gun's crew, but when I recovered I went to the boat deck where I found the Chief Officer, Second Officer, a Chinese carpenter and the Lascar Quartermaster, all on the port side. I assisted in lowering No. 2 boat, then, as the ship appeared to be all right, the Chief Officer told us to make the boat fast. I had four ribs broken and my back had been injured when I was thrown from the platform, so the Chief Officer told me I had better sit down and rest. I did so, and about fifteen minutes later there was a second explosion again on the starboard side, this time in the engine-room. The water pipe-line was shattered and water was flung everywhere. I immediately made a dash for the falls of No. 2 boat hoping to get it away, but while doing so the water rushed over the vessel and she went down within a minute of being struck.

I was sucked down with the ship and when I eventually came to the surface I managed to grab hold of some wreckage. I could see nobody, but after a while heard some shouts and then recognized the fourth officer's voice, so I called to him to ask him our position. He said he thought we were about 80 miles south of Freetown. We had no lights attached to our life-jackets, but saw various torches flashing in the water, so I thought some of the officers must be about. We carried six lifeboats, but none of these had been got away, and we had no large rafts, only two buoyant floats about 5ft. square, which were not fitted with lights. These floats are only meant to hang on to, and in this way will support about 20 men. I definitely think that had there been any rafts which would have floated off the ship more men would have been saved.

After about half-an-hour I saw what looked like the back of a person sitting on something, and this turned out to be one of the passengers, who had managed to scramble on to one of these small floats. I paddled over to him and climbed on. My ribs and back were hurting a bit, but not a lot at that time. Five minutes later we heard the voice of the second Radio Officer calling, we shouted to him, he swam towards us, and he too climbed on to the float. The float was not built to be sat on, the weight of three men almost submerged it, and we were sitting in water. Then we heard someone call out to the Chief Officer, and his reply, 'I have got an oar.' That is the last we heard of him. The sea was quite calm, and at this time we saw no sharks, the explosions probably having frightened them from the vicinity. Gradually the flashing torches drifted further away from us, then three Lascars drifted by us, we called out to them, and they said they were in a 'tank'. I do not know if these were the three Lascars who were picked up.

When dawn broke the sea was clear of wreckage, and we

three were alone on the float. We managed to pick up a broken oar, which was the only thing left from the ship. We had no food or water, as these floats are not meant to be used as rafts, and have no accommodation for supplies. It was a small wooden structure about 5 ft. square floating on four buoyancy tanks, and as I have said, we were sitting in the water all the time. On the fourth day, 3rd April, in the afternoon, we saw something in the distance which looked like a small ship lying directly in the path of the sun. The passenger took off his shirt and waved it, none of us was able to stand by this time, as we were too weak, and the signal was not seen. Then I remembered a cigarette case in my pocket, so I threw away the cigarettes, and the Radio Officer used the case as a heliograph to signal. After a while the object drew nearer, and we recognized the conning-tower of a submarine. It drew right alongside and we asked for some water. The Commander gave us about a gallon in a tin can, which tasted of fuel-oil and a few other things. He poured out a tumbler full of cognac, but we only had a mouthful each, and poured the rest into the can of water. We were already in a bad way as it had been very hot. I asked for something to eat, and we were given a tin of biscuits. All the time the Commander was talking to us photographs were being taken of us from the deck of the submarine. Suddenly the U-boat Commander sighted a ship, although we could see nothing, and he told us that if it was a neutral ship he would get them to pick us up, promising to return in half-an-hour. He steamed off on the surface and returned as promised in half-an-hour, but said nothing about the ship. The Commander asked if we were wounded, and where our lifeboats were, so I told him they had all been smashed by the second explosion. He raised a finger and said, 'I gave you 18 minutes to get your boats out. You are now some 30 miles off the shoals of Freetown, and have drifted 60 miles in four days, as when we torpedoed your ship you were 90 miles south of Freetown.' I asked him if he could take us in tow to bring us nearer land, but he said he was not allowed to do that; he asked if we were officers and receiving a negative reply, he remarked that if we had been officers he would have had to take us. My impression was that he would have liked to do more for us, but was frightened to do so, and I wondered if there were a Gestapo agent on board. He certainly seemed very friendly, and asked if there was anything else he could do for us, so I asked if he could give us something to use as paddles. He sent a seaman below who returned with four pieces of thin wood, but these were almost useless.

This officer was not a typical German, he was short, only about 5ft. 4in. tall, medium colouring and clean-shaven apart from a close-clipped moustache, aged about 35. He was wearing a black Scotch Glengarry cap, with the two ribbons at the back and a Scotch badge on it, a pair of trousers and a grey shirt. He spoke perfect English without the slightest trace of accent, and could easily have been an Englishman. I noticed 12 or 15 men standing on the conning tower, dressed in blue shorts with a white anchor embroidered on the left leg, nothing else. They were men of about 25, very bronzed, and looked very fit. They were big, well-made fellows, and made the Commander look quite small.

The submarine, which was not very large, was painted a greenish grey, and there was a Sunflower painted on the conning-tower, but no number. There were no slots or holes along the hull, but there was a metal shield about $\frac{7}{8}$ inch thick on either side of the hull amidships which was about 15 feet long and extended from deck level to well below the waterline. It stood slightly away from the vessel's side and I held on to it whilst we were talking. It was a one-piece conning-tower and had no canvas screen up; there was a gun forward of it and another smaller gun aft, there was no net-cutter or jumping wires.

We were alongside for about 15 minutes, then he pushed off, and we were left alone. We were in high spirits, thinking we were near land and should make it in a couple of days, and for this reason we had not asked for any more food or water. In any case, had we been given more food I doubt if we should have been able to keep it, as a nasty swell rose that night, and we lost the tin of biscuits after having eaten only one of them.

Nothing happened for two days after leaving the submarine, but on the third day, 6 April, we noticed a change in the colour of the water. It was slightly muddy, there was plant-life, and we thought we were getting near land, but nothing happened. One night we saw a hospital ship with all her lights on, and having been given some cigarettes and matches by the Germans, we tried to burn a shirt to make a flare, but the matches were damp, and the ship passed on. The following day we saw another ship about a mile away steering a zigzag course, and as we were lying to windward of her we all three shouted as loudly as we could, but they did not see or hear our signals. The next day a flying-boat appeared apparently flying straight towards us, and we thought he must see us; we waved frantically with pieces of clothing, but he failed to see our signals and flew overhead and away out of sight.

On the tenth day after having been torpedoed, the Wireless Operator died. The passenger and I were very weak by now, but he was a little better than I. He was a fairly strong young man, about 26 years old, and was returning home on leave from service with the Tanganyika Police Force; he had really kept us going so far. The days were terribly hot, and on the same day as the Operator died, 9th April, three days after leaving the submarine, the water was finished. Soon after this I began to suffer from hallucinations. I dreamed that I had had a cup of tea, and when I awoke I told the passenger I was going below for a cup of tea. I got off the raft and dived under, then he dragged me back and asked me what I had found. I said I had gone down the wrong way and promptly went over the side. Three times I did this, and each time he had a terrific struggle to get me back on to the float. After the third time the passenger said he was getting so weak that he would be unable to help me if I went off again, and I remained where I was after that. At that time, fortunately, there were no sharks about, but a little later there was not a day or night when we were not troubled by them. They would swim under the float and hump against it in an effort to throw us into the water, or they would come so close alongside that their large fins would scrape along the edge of the float. Many of them were about 12 feet long, and although we tried to strike them with the piece of wood the Germans had given us it had no effect as we were too weak to hit them very hard.

On 12 April, 13 days after being torpedoed, the passenger saw a ship. We had had nothing to drink for $5\frac{1}{2}$ days then, and by this time I was not interested in anything; I did not even bother to look up. The ship drew alongside, lowered a dinghy and we were taken on board. She was the British *Lorca*. We were in a pretty bad way by that time. I had used my lifejacket to sit on, but we were actually sitting in the water all the time, with spray breaking over us from the swell. I was covered with salt water sores and boils, and my ribs and back had been terribly painful. We had had only one biscuit in 13 days and no water for the last $5\frac{1}{2}$ days. We did not drink salt water, but I think it was this which killed the Radio Officer. We had no protection for our heads aginst the sun, so we used to dip our clothes in the water and put them on our heads to cool them, but it was so hot that the material dried in about five minutes. Fortunately most of the nights were warm, but we dreaded them as we knew that during the hours of darkness there was no hope of being found.

I learned later, when I recovered a little, that when the passenger sighted the vessel he had managed to wave his shirt, but was too weak to stand. We could only sit on the float with our knees drawn up to our chins. They must have had a very good look-out in the *Lorca* for he picked us up with his binoculars, but when he reported to her Captain, the float was so small, only five feet square, that they had some difficulty in finding us again. When we were picked up we were almost back in the position where our ship had been sunk, 90 miles from Freetown, so we must have got into the track of another current after leaving the submarine and been taken back. We were landed at Freetown on the 13th April. I had lost $3\frac{1}{2}$ stone in weight.

15

A Thirty-Five Hours' Swim

Leading Seaman C. de Wolf of the Royal Netherlands Navy describes the last voyage of HNM Submarine O.16, her successes off Patani and Kota Bharu where she sank four Japanese transports on 11 December, 1941, her loss by mining on 15 December and his own adventures before he was brought back to Singapore on 21 December.

Saturday, 6 December. We left Singapore, in the direction of the Gulf of Siam. Spirits on board were excellent, increased alertness was noticeable, four men were allowed fresh air on the bridge at a time, and the sea was calm. During the night of Monday/Tuesday (9/10 December) we met two Japanese destroyers, they turned their searchlights on us and we dived to 130 feet, but apparently they had not seen us as they only steamed slowly up and down. The war had begun, but on board this was not known. During the day we stayed submerged, at 1900 we emptied tank III and proceeded in a northerly direction. At 1900 we heard the Governor-General's speech, and knew from this that the war had begun. All necessary measures were taken and we were prepared for our task. During the day men not keeping watch slept. Action stations were occupied when the ship was submerged.

Thursday, 11 December. At about 2000, while we were submerged, a Japanese transport came into sight. Helmsmen were at action stations, everything went calmly, no one was nervous. The freighter was sailing in the direction of Patani, we proceeded trimmed at six metres depth for 10 miles. The Japanese freighter sailed into the bay, lights were burning on the coast, which helped us to gauge our position. Mr. E. was navigating, and at 2130 the freighter lowered anchor, then we discovered that three other ships were lying there fully laden. The Captain ordered the preparation of the bow and stern tubes, and we approached on the electric motor.

There was only five fathoms of water, so diving was out of the question. The Captain brought the submarine into position, and there followed a succession of six explosions. Loud cheers came from the bridge and also from the control-room, and we returned in the direction from which we had come. When four miles out the diesels were started and tank III emptied. At 2300 we celebrated our success with a glass of wine. In the control-room, which served as smoking-room, our action was also toasted. Everyone congratulated the Captain on his success. After this everyone with no watch to keep retired to rest.

In the morning a Japanese merchantman came in sight, we had one torpedo in the tank. When the Second in Command said 'Boys, another Jap!' the torpedo was out of the tank and in the tube in next to no time, but alas, we lost her on account of a thick rain storm into which we ran. We proceeded further, course Singapore. There is not much to tell of these days, during daylight submerged, on the surface at about 1900, the last two days emptied tanks II and III for more speed.

Sunday, 14 December. I have the dog watch, sit until 2000 in the control-room and then go to my berth. Bosun N. has the first watch. At midnight when I come on the bridge, the weather is good, but horizon hazy, the Bosun had just been relieved by the Second in Command. The Captain is also on the bridge, because since 2330 searchlights have been seen, and now and then gun flashes. The Bosun goes below, the Captain stays, we joke on the bridge over the fools who show their searchlights.

At 0200 the searchlight comes over the horizon from direction 165. We steer course 210, right on to the searchlight, the islands should now come into sight, every 20 minutes the light flashes, with growing excitement we follow the course. The horizon is clearer. There are six of us on the bridge, the Captain, the Second in Command, myself and three others.

Suddenly at about 0230 a terrific crash, and I see the ship split in two at about the height of the deck tubes, a huge column of water sweeps over the bridge followed by the smell of diesel oil. The Captain and Second in Command try to kick the conning-tower hatch shut, but fail. My raincoat is caught in the anti-mine wires, but I manage to get it loose. The ship sinks in less than a minute, and I find myself in the water.

I look round and find nothing, I call and get a reply. Further away the others are floating, I swim to them and see that they are all there except the Captain. We called him and heard an answering call, but he could not get to us, was probably too far off, and I have never seen him again.

I asked the Second in Command if he knew the cause of the explosion, he said that it was probably a mine. He explained to us where we were, and it turned out that if we wished to swim to the islands we must keep the moon on our left and a certain star on our right. We swam on together; Able Seaman T. could not go much further, we had pulled off our clothes but T. had on a short coat that he could not pull off, and it hampered him. I could not bear to see this and swam back to him, to help him; this was successful. Daylight began to come; soon after this T. gave up and sank. Right on the horizon we perceived the islands, I kept on encouraging the others to swim on, but at about 0800 the Second in Command sank. I asked B. and K. how they were getting on, the answer was – 'thirsty'. Now we could see the mountain tops of the islands, we should soon be saved. A plane passed over us but did not spot us. At 0900 Able Seaman K. sank; I know the time exactly because my watch went until 1000, then it stopped; by then B. and I were alone. We swam on but I noticed that the current carried us east of the island, we swam against it until we were once more before the island, then it carried us further away again. At about 1700, when the sun went down we were overcome by a terrible thirst. B. said to me – 'C., I can't go any further, if you get through alive take messages to my wife and two children', after this he sank. I still swam on, with more strength, but I was constantly carried away by the treacherous current. At last on

Tuesday, 16 December, at about 0100, after having swum

for 35 hours, I reached the island. I was thrown on the rocks, where I lay, bleeding heavily from my back and legs. After some time scorching heat of the sun on my body, pain in my legs and a terrific thirst brought me to myself, and to the knowledge that I must have water. That was the most important thing.

For about five hours I wandered about the island, but without result, there was no water there, I fell every now and then, stood up again, the thorns scratched my whole body. Now that I knew there was no water up here I decided to return to the rocks, to spend the night. As I clambered down again I found a cleft in the rocks, from which water flowed. I lay there and drank, and fell afterwards into a restless sleep, waking every now and then. When the sun rose above the horizon I tried to walk round the island, this was not easy as my path took me over rocks from eighteen to twenty feet high. After long climbing and clambering I at last reached the side of the island. Here to my great joy I saw a proa; I called as loud as I could, the native in the boat heard me and came in his small craft towards me. I signed to him that he must come to me over the rocks. I asked with signs for drink and food. A minute later he brought me a cocoa-nut, and showed me that I must go with him in his little boat, and this I did. He gave me his vest, and an hour later I was on one of the other islands. All the inhabitants gathered to have a look at me. I was given a pair of trousers, at least, what had been a pair of trousers, and thus I was led before the head of the native village. He spoke Malay, so I could explain all that had happened. I was very well received, was given a plate of sago with rice and water, at night I slept on the ground, and in the morning I sat before the door of my new home. A conference was held, and it was decided that I should leave on

Saturday, 20 December, at 0800 in a sailing proa for Tanggaro on my way to Singapore. The sea was fairly rough, but after nine hours' sailing we lay off Tanggaro. We could not land, as four miles of uncovered mud banks lay between us and the quay, so we had to wait until 1800. Then we sailed up the river and moored at the edge of the wood. I slept that night in the proa. The next day

Sunday, 21 December, while it was still dark, we began to unrig the proa, for I understood that the natives who had sailed over with me were to take me to Jemolengan, this was the nearest station where there were Australian troops. I imagined that the road would be rather like the Malang road, but I should soon find out. We came before the Headman of Tanggaro, and after having drunk coffee, we began our journey by first walking along the beach. Very soon my feet became scratched and torn by the shells and sharp stones, but it was to become much worse before very long. On the way we met twelve Chinese, who were on the way to Mersing, a place further on than our destination. So, with a Chinese as guide, we started off into the unknown, and turning right entered the jungle. There was no path, nothing but branches and trees, through which we had to cut our way. We passed through morasses into which we sank up to our waists, and our speed was probably about $2\frac{1}{2}$ kilometres per hour. With each step I took I cried out with pain. Now and then the sun broke through the trees. Silently we went on. I had to rest often on the way, and by noon could go no further. Everyone waited until I could go on again. I often asked how much longer the journey would take, but no one could give me an answer.

The Chinese who had first acted as a guide had returned to Tanggaro, after having given the usual signs and salutations. Now three Malays were acting as guides, and they were ahead, making a path.

At 1300 I saw the Malays sitting in a tree, and through the branches I saw a brown sunburnt face with black hair, and in front of this face a long bayonet. At first I was startled, but then realized that it must be one of the troops. I could have cried out with gladness. I walked up to him with my hands up, and told him that I was a Dutchman from the submarine. I explained everything to him, and we were taken to the camp.

Here I was very well received. They gave me food and tea, my feet were cleansed and they gave me shoes. The Chinese and Malays were examined, and they detailed two soldiers to take me to the Australian camp. After having walked another eight kilometres I at last arrived, dead tired in body and spirit, in the camp. Here I had a very hearty reception, was again given food, my feet were once more given attention, they gave me cigarettes, a bath and shaved me, presented me with an Australian suit and four dollars, and when all this had happened I was led before an Australian officer, who interrogated me. Then I was taken before another Australian officer, and later before the Commandant of the Australian troops. When this was finished I travelled in a luxurious Ford V8 car with an officer and two soldiers on the way to Singapore. At 1800 we reached a station, where I was questioned by an English Major; I still spoke Malay as this was the easiest language for us both. I was put into another car and set out once more for Singapore, where at 1900 I was in the ward-room of the Naval Base. Here the officer who brought me to Singapore did all the talking. A little later I was taken to the Officers' Long Room, where I was given food. I had to wait for a Dutch officer from one of the submarines, who had been warned that I was here. At 2000 Mr. W. came and took me to the submarine barracks. I was taken into the sick bay. A doctor was fetched, he examined me and told me that the one cure for me was much rest and good food.

Monday, 22 December. When I woke up, the boys from the K-11 and K-13 were by my bed, I talked to them, and later was fetched by an officer, as I had to report to Colonel K. I told him my story. After this I had to go to the Admiral of Singapore, who was very pleased with my report, and thanked me for it, as it was, according to him, of great value. The Colonel brought me to the *Janssens*, on board of which ship I left Singapore in the afternoon.

16

The Chinaman's Wristwatch

On Saturday, 21 November 1942, Poon Lim, the Chinese second steward of the British *Benlomond*, 6,630 tons, asked the First Officer when they would reach the next port, Paramaribo in Dutch Guiana. He was told, 'On Saturday or Sunday next.' As the *Benlomond* was torpedoed on Monday the 23rd, he calculated that she was six days away from her destination, for which she had sailed from Capetown in ballast thirteen days earlier. That is all he knows about the ship's position when sunk.

It was at 11.45 on Monday, 23 November, that he felt and heard a big explosion from the direction of the engine room. He was in his room at the time, grabbed his life-belt and put it on while running down the alley along the saloon and towards his boat-station. When he got there he found two of the officers and one seaman trying to lower the life-boat. He joined them and they had just raised her off the chocks when he was washed away by a green sea. He was carried deep under and when his life-belt brought him to the surface he could no longer see the *Benlomond* nor any trace of her except some planks floating round him. He got hold of one of these and paddled about until he came across a life-raft, swam towards it and climbed on to it. He was then able to look round and saw another raft, but so far away that he could not recognize the four men on it. He thinks they were the gun-crew, who had been on deck by their gun. These men waved to him to join them, but he could not get his raft to move, being alone on it. He states that he saw no other

members of the crew but did hear several calling out and
crying for help. Later the two rafts were drawn apart and he
lost sight of the other.

About this time he saw a submarine at some distance. She
was on the surface when he saw her first and remained so,
while moving away and disappearing.

On the raft Poon Lim found water and food stored which
sufficed for him for fifty days. He drifted about without being
able to direct or move the raft. He saw several ships, one quite
close to him. For this one he fired a flare he found on the raft,
but the ship did not respond and steamed on. Before the fifty
days were up he managed to dig a nail out of a plank of the
raft with his teeth, and with the same tools formed it into a
fish-hook. He unravelled the life line round the raft and made
a fishing line. He baited his hook with some biscuit, made into
a paste, and soon caught a fish which resembled a whiting.
This he used to bait for bigger fish, and caught some
eventually as heavy as 'fifty pounds.' It may be deduced that
by this time the currents had brought him in nearer to South
America or the mouth of the Amazon. He also caught
sea-gulls which settled on the raft while he was lying down
between the benches, over which he spread the material of his
life-belt as a protection from the sun and to catch rain-water.
He was washed by sea-water all the time and was stark naked.
He was burned on shoulders, back and arms to a deep
black-brown, but did not blister and showed no salt-water
sores, although when found he was scratched and showed
signs of old scars. When his water ran out he was able to
gather enough rain-water to fill the tins. It rained very often,
which also seems to show he was not far off the Brazilian coast
at the time. For five days only did he have to go without water.
This occurred after he had been one hundred days on the raft,
and he seems to have suffered then the worst anxiety of all his
130 days on the raft. He also saw several aircraft, again
showing that he must have been drifting some time along the
Brazilian coast. One came right down to inspect him and in
fact did report him to the U.S. Naval authorities at Belem.
Another aircraft went out to search for him but did not find
the raft.

At last a Brazilian negro fisherman sighted him some ten miles out to sea off the coast east of Salinas in the State of Parà. This man sailed out to the raft and picked him up. He had to be lifted off the raft as he was too weak to get up. He was overjoyed and sang and laughed and ate voraciously. The fisherman particularly observed that he ate red pepper, of very powerful pepperiness, by the handful and seemed to enjoy the bite or not notice it. Three days later, on 5th April, he landed at Belem, able to walk and amazingly agile, although very weak. He was taken charge of by the British Consul and put to bed in hospital under the doctor's care. The doctor reported that he was in need of rest and building-up with tonics and that the only thing really wrong with him otherwise was a derangement of the stomach, probably due to the raw food which he had eaten for so long and to exposure. A fortnight later he was up and about and fit to be returned to the United Kingdom. Almost at once after his rescue he had expressed the desire to return to duty. He was very fond, it seems, of his Captain in the *Benlomond* and was upset by the certainty now acquired of the latter's death. Poon Lim became a favourite at the Beneficiença Portuguesa Hospital, where the nuns, who did not at first like the idea of taking charge of a Chinese, all became delighted with him. He had lost all he had, of course, and in particular a wrist-watch. The British colony at Belem, however, subscribed to present him with a new one, with inscription all complete.

Bibliography and Notes

1. St Paul on Melita
Taken from the Holy Bible, Acts of the Apostles 27-28:10, in the Revised Version (1881).

The island on which St Paul was wrecked is, by tradition, the outermost of the two islets to the north of St Paul's Bay on the north coast of Malta. This island is used every summer for grazing sheep, and a chapel was built on it during the 1960s.

2. An Elizabethan Sailor
Strange and Wonderfull Things. Happened to Richard Hasleton, borne at Braintree in Essex. In his ten yeares travailes in many forraine countries. Penned as he delivered it FROM HIS OWNE MOUTH ... London, 1595, with its accompanying woodcuts, said to be by the Italian engraver Poliphilus, is now an exceedingly rare book; even the British Museum can offer only a microfilm of the copy in the Huntington Library, California, which appears to have been acquired by purchase from a private English source in 1919, for £66. The illustration from the first edition of the book appears here by courtesy of the Huntington Library. Long extracts from *Strange and Wonderfull Things* ... were printed in *The English Garner*, volume 4, edited by Edward Arber (1903).

3. A Long and Disconsolate Captivity
An Historical Relation of the Island of Ceylon by Robert Knox first appeared from the Royal Society's printer in 1681 and was instantly successful, German, Dutch and French editions appearing within the next decade. King Charles II much admired it and gave the author an audience. The best modern edition, with a portrait, map and the original plates, was published by the Ceylon Historical Society, with an introduction by S.D. Saparmadu, in 1958.

136

4. Young Drury

Artless and confused, *The Pleasant and Surprising Adventures of Robert Drury during his Fifteen Years on the Island of Madagascar, Written by Himself*, was first published in 1729, twelve years after his return to London, with a second edition in 1743. The bald summary of it given here conveys little of the riches of a true-life story which leaves Marryat and Ballantyne standing at the post; little of the hardships he surmounted, or the high spirits of the author, who combined resourcefulness and an extremely tough physique with a talent for practical jokes, mainly at the expense of local witch-doctors. So exceptional were his experiences that clever literary men were from the start inclined to refuse to accept the book at its face value, though Madagascar experts have always done so, citing the detailed vocabulary with which it concludes, and the brief endorsement from Captain Mackett, Drury's rescuer, which appears at the start. It is true that the disquisitions on local religion and laws are rather more than one would expect a publican's son to manage out of his own head; true also that the 1743 edition speaks casually of an 'editor'. However, expert scrutiny of the elaborate Malagasy vocabulary in phonetic spelling attached to the book led Rev. J. Richardson of the London Missionary Society's school in Tananarive to conclude that this part of the book at least had been dictated verbally in response to his editor's prompting – so persistent and consistent are his cockney-style corruptions of the various Malagasy consonants; and it seems possible that the whole was strung together from informal conversations, rather than from any written account. Long and scholarly papers have been written both for and against the idea that Daniel Defoe might have been the editor in question.

5. The *Wager*

The four books are (1) *The Narrative of the Honourable John Byron, containing an account of the great distresses suffered by himself and his companions on the coast of Patagonia, from the year 1740, till their arrival in England 1746* – London 1768; (2) John Bulkeley & John Cummins: *A Voyage to the South Seas by H.M. Ship Wager* – London 1743. (3) Alexander Campbell: *The Sequel to Bulkeley and Cummins's Voyage to the South Seas* – Printed for the Author 1747. (4) *A Narrative of the dangers and distresses which befel Isaac Morris, and seven more of the crew belonging to the Wager Store-Ship, which attended Captain Anson in his voyage to the South Sea* – London 1750 (?)

Note that the Byron account was written more than twenty years after the events described.

6. Russians on Spitzbergen
From the German narrative first published in 1768 by M. Le Roy,
professor of history in St Petersburg.

7. Trading with the Natives
From the account of the wreck of the *Doddington* in *Shipwrecks &
Disasters at Sea* (1812).

8. Damsel in Distress
From the account of the loss of the *Catharine, Venus* and *Piedmont* in
Shipwrecks & Disasters at Sea (1812).

9. The Cannibals
From 'Sufferings of Six Deserters' in *Shipwrecks & Disasters at Sea*
(1812).

10. Amazing Grace
This account is based on *The Journals of William Darling*, edited by
Grace's elder sister Thomasin and published in London in 1886, 20
years after Darling's death; also on reports of the inquest held at
Bamburgh four days after the wreck published in the *Newcastle
Journal* and its rival the *Gateshead Observer*. The Berwick *Warder* office
issued a memoir of Grace in 1843, and the full biography by
Constance Smedley (1932) is essential for those who wish to follow
the last four years of Grace's life. Leslie Gardiner has contributed
many helpful suggestions over matters of detail.
  For other good general accounts see Christopher Nicholson: *Rock
Lighthouses of Britain* (1983), which includes photographs; Oliver
Warner: *The Lifeboat Service* (1974) and Patrick Howarth: *The Lifeboat
Story* (1957).

11. A Victorian in the Arctic
The two books by Trevor-Battye are *Icebound on Kolguev* (1895) and *A
Northern Highway of the Tsar* (1898), the latter a *locus classicus* for all
that is good and bad in the Russian character. I have received
further help from Mrs Peter Le Breton, Trevor-Battye's daughter.
The article first appeared in *The Cornhill* of Spring 1974.

12. 3,400 Miles in Open Boats
Condensed from C.P.T. Foster: *1700 Miles in Open Boats* – another
rare book, the publisher having gone out of business shortly after.
Since there were two boats sailing separately for most of the time, I

have taken the liberty of doubling the *1700 Miles* of the original book title.

Rodriguez has had a chequered history. First known to Portuguese navigators as Diego Ruys, it was colonized in 1691 by a party of eight Huguenot bachelors, exiles from Europe, who had the idea of settling there for life, but were defeated by boredom and the absence of females, and after two years set sail in desperation for Mauritius which they reached after nine days in their hand-made open boat. The book by their leader François Leguat (1708) gave the first detailed account of the appearance and habits of the Dodo, a kind of flightless super-pigeon, altogether too fanciful for home-based naturalists to swallow; nevertheless it was from deep caves on Rodriguez that in the 1890s the first cache of dodo bones was recovered, enabling the first skeleton of the beast (*Pezophaps Solitaria*) to be reconstructed – this is still to be seen in the Port Louis museum.

During the next century there were occasional visits by naturalists and some desultory settlement by adventurous families, the Mathurins giving their name to the overgrown village, Port Mathurin, which is still the island's capital. In 1810, at the end of the Napoleonic Wars, a British expeditionary force from India used the island as a base for operations against the French in Mauritius and Réunion. In 1874 some British astronomers aboard HMS *Shearwater* lugged their telescopes ashore and converted the place into one of the nine British observation stations for the Transit of Venus in November of that year.

A devastating cyclone swept Rodriguez in April 1886, followed by months of drought. The inhabitants, by then totalling 1,700, decided to seek help from the outer world to avoid starvation, so set off for Mauritius in an open boat to get rice from the authorities. From 1901 to 1970 Rodriguez was a British cable station on the line from Durban to Australia, supporting a resident European staff of twenty. The island followed its larger neighbour into independence in 1968, remaining a member of the British Commonwealth under HM the Queen, who visited her island in March 1972. From 1973 onwards a thrice-weekly scheduled air service by Air Mauritius has supplemented the somewhat erratic arrangements of the monthly mail boat from Port Louis, and done as much as anything to drag the island forward into the twentieth century.

The inhabitants of the island today number some 35,000 – a far cry from those eight bachelors of 1691.

13. An Italian in the Red Sea

From RN Intelligence sources. Translated from an Italian submarine engineer's diary left behind on an island in the Red Sea on which he was a castaway in 1940. It is not known whether he survived his ultimate rescue.

For this story and the remaining three in the book I have been much helped by David Brown of the MOD/Naval Historical Branch. All four are Crown Copyright, used by permission.

14. Four Broken Ribs

From RN Intelligence sources. E.G. Elliott, a merchant seaman gunner survived – with one passenger and three lascars out of a total complement of 99 – from a British merchant ship, the *Umona*, 3767 tons, torpedoed between Walvis Bay and Freetown.

15. A Thirty-Five Hours' Swim

From RN Intelligence sources. Leading Seaman C. de Wolf of the Royal Netherlands Navy gave this account of his adventures after the Dutch submarine 0.16 was mined off Malaya on December 15th 1941.

16. The Chinaman's Wristwatch

From RN Intelligence sources. Poon Lim was a Chinese steward on the British *Benlomond*, 6,630 tons, torpedoed in 1942 13 days out from Cape Town on a voyage to Paramaribo in Dutch Guiana. He later received the MBE.